Discounting and Intergenerational Equity

Edited by
Paul R. Portney and John P. Weyant

Resources for the Future
Washington, DC

Printed in the United States of America

Published by Resources for the Future
1616 P Street, NW, Washington, DC 20036–1400

Library of Congress Cataloging-in-Publication Data

Discounting and intergenerational equity / edited by Paul R. Portney and John P. Weyant
      p.   cm.
      Includes bibliographical references and index.
      ISBN 0–915707–89–6

    1. Policy sciences.   2. Cost effectiveness.   3. Intergenerational relations. 4. Social justice. I. Portney, Paul R. II. Weyant, John P. (John Peter).
H97.D57   1999
320'.6—dc21   98–31878
                                                        CIP

The paper in this book meets the guidelines for permanence and durability of the Committee on Production Guidelines for Book Longevity of the Council on Library Resources.

This book was typeset in Palatino by Betsy Kulamer; its cover was designed by AURAS Design.

About
Resources for the Future

Resources for the Future is an independent nonprofit organization engaged in research and public education with issues concerning natural resources and the environment. Established in 1952, RFF provides knowledge that will help people to make better decisions about the conservation and use of such resources and the preservation of environmental quality.

RFF has pioneered the extension and sharpening of methods of economic analysis to meet the special needs of the fields of natural resources and the environment. Its scholars analyze issues involving forests, water, energy, minerals, transportation, sustainable development, and air pollution. They also examine, from the perspectives of economics and other disciplines, such topics as government regulation, risk, ecosystems and biodiversity, climate, Superfund, technology, and outer space.

Through the work of its scholars, RFF provides independent analysis to decisionmakers and the public. It publishes the findings of their research as books and in other formats, and communicates their work through conferences, seminars, workshops, and briefings. In serving as a source of new ideas and as an honest broker on matters of policy and governance, RFF is committed to elevating the public debate about natural resources and the environment.

Contents

Foreword

In some circles, economists have the reputation of being unimaginative bean-counters, doggedly claiming to quantify the unquantifiable (or to eff the ineffable?), and perfectly personifying Oscar Wilde's definition of a cynic as someone who knows the price of everything and the value of nothing. It seems to me that no one who reads this book with care could go along with that judgment.

Here are twenty mainstream economists tackling a genuinely deep and difficult problem: how should one compare and evaluate policies whose effects can be expected to stretch out over long periods of time—centuries or more—and many generations? I doubt that there can ever be a neat and convincing general answer to that question, but even approximate and partial insights would count for a lot. These economists are certainly not insensitive to the subtleties and ambivalences and ethical nuances that come with the territory. It is true that they would give a lot for a rough quantitative answer; but that only reflects the fact that any policy can be pushed harder or less hard, further or less far, and that a useful evaluation has to suggest how hard and how far. The beans have to be counted, if only approximately: those gentle souls who merely ooh and ah over them are arguably part of the problem, not part of the solution.

Not many readers will remember Alben Barkley, who was a U.S. senator from Kentucky and later Harry Truman's vice president. Some fifty years ago, I heard him speak at Harvard. He told the story of a country preacher whose congregation came to inform him that he was being fired. "Why do you do that," he complained. "Didn't I magnify, didn't I glorify, didn't I terrify?" "Yes, you did," replied the leader of the congregation. "You magnified, you glorified, you terrified. But you didn't tell us wherein, and we want a preacher who will tell us wherein." The least you can say for these economists is that they try to tell us wherein.

When asked to summarize and evaluate costs and benefits over time, it is second nature for any economist to reach for a discount rate, and very likely a market interest rate. There are many cases, especially on the cost side, where that is the right thing to do. If a dollar's worth of resources today can be invested to yield $(1 + I)^{10}$ dollars worth of roughly equivalent resources ten years from today, without much else changing, then costs of $(1 + I)^{10}$ dollars to be incurred in ten years count for only a dollar today. As everyone knows, however, there are cases, especially on the benefit (or damage) side, when discounting at anything like market interest rates implies conclusions that common sense can not accept. Even very large damages, if they will happen 200 years from now, discount back to peanuts.

One possible escape is to argue that the "right" year-to-year discount rate gets smaller and smaller as the years we are comparing recede into the distant future. Martin Weitzman gives reasons, in the afterthoughts to his chapter (Chapter 3), why this might be appropriate. It is also implied by the "hyperbolic discounting" of Maureen Cropper and David Laibson (Chapter 16). But this suggestion solves one problem by creating another. Unless the discount rate is constant, the policy path is subject to "time inconsistency." Suppose an intelligent decisionmaker plans a strategy for the long future, beginning today. Five years from now, she reconsiders the strategy, having followed it so far. She will want to change to a different strategy, for no other reason than the passage of time. And in another five (or four or three or two) years, she will want to change again, and she will know that she will want to violate the current strategy.

This sounds like a poor way to run a railroad. Cropper and Laibson, and Kenneth Arrow in Chapter 2, suggest that we follow an old solution of Edmund Phelps and Robert Pollak and regard successive generations—or decades or years—as playing a noncooperative game. Then, the best strategy that can actually be carried out, since no generation can alter the past or commit its successors, is an equilibrium of that game. Leaving aside all technical points, I have to say that this does not feel anything like the way policy is talked about or could be talked about in a democracy, especially since any current generation is notoriously bad at guessing what future generations will want or do.

Thomas Schelling proposes a more radical thought (in Chapter 10), with which I have a lot of sympathy. The whole notion of discounting benefits or satisfactions is rooted in the idea of time preference or degrees of impatience. There are grasshoppers and there are ants; some licorice-lovers hoard the black jelly beans, and others eat them all right away. If today's policy choice is made to depend on the relative weight attached to benefits 150 years from today and to those enjoyed 1,225 years from today, just whose impatience are we supposed to be reflecting? Certainly not yours or mine. We have neither the capacity nor the right to make such judgments, especially because—as Schelling points out—the beneficiaries may well be people living in distant parts of the world, about whom we know nothing, and for whose ancestors—our contemporaries—we seem to care very little. The usual rationale begins to seem a bit ridiculous.

This feeling is reinforced by another inescapable reflection. The fact is that we—those making or voting on policy decisions today—know almost nothing about the technological and economic possibilities that will be available 200 years from now. This is not so much a matter of uncertainty or of sheer ignorance or even of vocabulary. One device that is appropriate in some bits of economics is to reflect uncertainty by deeper discounting. But that seems quite inappropriate here: we want to allow for the fact that we don't know, not that we don't care. The right notion may be something like a diffuse prior, in Bayesian terms, only more so.

In any case, William Nordhaus's wise admonition, derived from economic calculation, is relevant here (and elsewhere): it is far better to think through what you are trying to accomplish, and then do it—or at least aim at it—directly than it is to fudge the discount rate and spoil other parts of the policy.

All this leads me to a concluding thought. Maybe the idea of a unitary decisionmaker—like an optimizing individual or a wise and impartial adviser—is not very helpful when it comes to the choice of policies that will have distant-future effects about which one can now know hardly anything. Serious policy choice may then be a different animal, quite unlike individual saving and investment decisions. Those responsible for such decisions may meet in a frame of mind that should not be analogized to the choice of a meal from a restaurant menu. "Responsibility" suggests something less personal. What would Edmund Burke say, or Charles James Fox, about such choices? I think they would like to read this book before telling us wherein.

ROBERT M. SOLOW
Institute Professor of Economics
Massachusetts Institute of Technology
Nobel Laureate in Economic Science

Discounting and
Intergenerational Equity

1

Introduction

Paul R. Portney and John P. Weyant

The stars would appear to be in alignment once again with regard to discounting—the technique by which economists and other policy analysts attempt to compare the immediate effects of policy changes (both pro and con) with those occurring in the more distant future. At least two sets of events are interacting to elevate, once again, the visibility of this arcane and often misunderstood, but also quite important, subject.

The first of these events is the international debate about climate change. Many scientists, environmentalists, politicians, and others favor strong action to slow the accumulation of carbon dioxide and the other gases that trap outgoing or terrestrial radiation and, thus, have the potential to warm the earth's atmosphere (the so-called *greenhouse effect*). Even proponents of immediate action, however, readily acknowledge two things. First, the most serious adverse effects that might attend global warming would not occur for decades at the least, and more likely centuries from now. Second, actions taken today to begin addressing this problem will give rise to costs in the here and now. This necessitates some way of comparing, at least qualitatively, these near-term costs with more distant benefits.

Of course, global climate change is not the only problem for which solutions present this pattern of benefits and costs. Within the environmental field alone, both radioactive waste disposal and the preservation of biodiversity have similar profiles of benefits and costs. In the case of the former, the lion's share of the cost of identifying and building a waste disposal site must be incurred up front. Because of the extraordinarily long half-life of radioactive wastes, however, the benefits of safe disposal

PAUL R. PORTNEY is president and senior fellow at Resources for the Future. JOHN P. WEYANT is director of the Energy Modeling Forum and a professor in the Department of Engineering–Economic Systems at Stanford University.

will be felt for tens if not hundreds of thousands of years. For the latter, the costs associated with preserving biodiversity (which often take the form of development benefits forgone) are incurred in the here and now; because once a species is lost, it is lost forever, most of the benefits of successfully preserving it will accrue to later generations. As with climate change, both problems force us to confront how much we are willing to sacrifice today for benefits that will be enjoyed later in our lives or in the lives of succeeding generations.

The growing attention devoted to these types of problems brings us to the second set of events moving discounting back into the policy limelight. Since the late 1970s, and particularly since 1994 when the Republican Party regained control of the U.S. Congress, interest has been growing in expanding the role of benefit-cost analysis (BCA) in federal regulation of the environment, occupational safety and health, and consumer products. (For an excellent history of such efforts and a description of the effects BCA has had on environmental regulation, see Morgenstern 1997.) The spate of regulatory reform legislation introduced in the last five years alone has forced economists and other proponents of BCA to think hard about how it might be applied constructively in rulemakings—especially for the more "exotic" kinds of problems discussed immediately above. At the same time, these legislative debates have positively energized opponents of BCA to focus on its problematic aspects—with valuation and discounting at the very top of the list. For this reason, too, then, discounting is being discussed outside the rather narrow academic circles in which it typically arises.

A TEMPORARY CONSENSUS

This is not the first time, however, that discounting has caught the attention of policymakers. Beginning with the first world oil market upheaval in 1973, the United States and other countries were forced to confront the possibility of making major changes in the ways in which they obtained energy. Among the many policy options under consideration were massive investments in new sources of supply, including the development of very large synthetic fuels plants. Because such facilities would entail huge upfront investments to produce benefits that would not begin to be realized for a number of years (and even then would be spread out over many years), discounting began to attract attention outside of the relatively small group of academics who thought about the comparison of benefits and costs across time.

In 1977, with the support and encouragement of the Electric Power Research Institute (EPRI), Resources for the Future (RFF) convened a conference to discuss the discount rate that ought to be used to evaluate government investments in energy and other technologies. Many of the leading thinkers of the day on this subject were commissioned to write papers; others participated in the conference as discussants or observers.

Nearly four years later, the revised papers, along with a significant contribution by Robert Lind (originally intended only to be a primer to accompany the other papers), were published as a book by RFF (Lind 1982). While the papers in this landmark volume were significant in their own right, it is fair to say that Lind's primer came to assume great importance. This was due in large part to a compromise he proposed in the book on the selection of a discount rate, the origins of which could be traced to Eckstein (1958), Diamond (1968), Feldstein (1970), and especially Bradford (1975). For all intents and purposes, Lind's proposed approach appeared to end at least temporarily disputes about discounting that had gone on for some time. In fact, for fifteen years or so after the publication of the book, when the question "What discount rate should be used to calculate the present value of benefits and costs?" was posed, the standard answer was a brief: "See Lind."

It isn't necessary to attempt here a thorough review of the competing views in 1977 about the appropriate discount rate. Lind's primer performs that service superbly. Similarly, no effort will be made here to spell out in great detail the compromise that Lind proposed. Briefly, though, he pulled together and expressed particularly clearly three important themes that by that time had emerged from the discounting debate. First, to the extent possible, all future benefits and costs should be converted to equivalent changes in consumption for the individuals who will experience them. Second, to the extent that the costs (benefits) of a public investment or regulatory program displace (augment) private capital formation, their consumption-equivalent measure should be adjusted upward to reflect the marginal productivity of capital. And third, these adjusted streams of consumption equivalents should be discounted using the social rate of time preference (or the rate at which society is willing to trade off present for future consumption). Those interested in a fuller and clearer explanation are directed to the book.

In the mid-1990s, however, Lind's apparent compromise seemed to unravel. As part of the ongoing deliberations of the Intergovernmental Panel on Climate Change (IPCC),[1] in 1995 a report was issued that dealt with, among other things, the economic and social ramifications of climate change and policies to address it (IPCC 1995). One chapter of this report was devoted to discounting and intergenerational equity (Arrow and others 1996). While the authors of this very influential chapter cited Lind's 1982 book frequently (among many other references), they made no pretense that a general agreement had been reached on discounting.

Indeed, in their discussion of discounting in benefit-cost analysis, they chose to organize their work by recognizing two opposing schools of thought on the selection of a discount rate, and they made no effort to reconcile the two.

Arrow and others referred to these two schools of thought as the *prescriptive* and the *descriptive* approaches. Under the former, the selection of the discount rate proceeds from what the authors call "ethical principles," or rules relating to the way that the well-being of different generations ought to be weighed. Under the latter, the choice of a discount rate is based on an observation of the rate(s) of return to capital invested in a variety of alternative assets.[2] Arrow and others suggest that the prescriptive approach will result in the selection of a lower discount rate than would result from the use of the descriptive approach.[3] Once again, or so it seemed, those looking for guidance on the choice of a discount rate could find justification for a rate at or near zero, as high as 20% and any and all values in between.

Into this breach once again stepped RFF, this time with Stanford University's Energy Modeling Forum (EMF). With support from EPRI, the U.S. Environmental Protection Agency, and the Department of Energy, RFF and EMF sponsored a workshop that brought together many of the world's best thinkers on discounting, including several who had participated in the conference that RFF had organized nearly two decades before. Climate change was the example that motivated much of the discussion at the workshop, although the conclusions regarding discounting can be generalized to all intergenerational decisionmaking.

Rather than ask the invited participants to write whatever they wanted about the selection of a discount rate, we decided to pose a common set of questions to those writing papers. Specifically, each author was asked the following questions.

- Should projects whose effects will be spread out over hundreds of years or more be treated simply as "longer versions" of projects whose principal effects extend no more than, say, thirty or forty years?
- If the answer to the above question is "yes," what is the appropriate way to determine the discount rate to be used?
- If projects with significant intergenerational effects are to be valued differently, how should this be done? Should benefits and costs in the distant future not be discounted at all? At a different rate?
- Perhaps more fundamentally, is it appropriate to use benefit-cost analysis at all in decisionmaking on such issues as climate change, disposal of high-level nuclear wastes, and so on?

As readers of this volume will see, some of the conferees dealt rather straightforwardly with these questions, while others addressed them only by implication. No attempt will be made in this introduction to sum-marize the papers, all of which were revised, some quite substantially, in the wake of the conference. Some chapters are long, others short. Some are quite technical, others not at all so—but in each chapter, the message of the author(s) or of those commenting on their work will be clear to interested readers.

KEY POINTS

Having attended the workshop, discussed the issues with the partici-pants, read and re-read each of the papers, and thought long and hard about discounting, we have several observations to offer to readers of this volume.

First, it is impossible to read these papers without getting a sense of the unease even the best minds in the profession feel about discounting, due to the technical complexity of the issues and to their ethical ramifica-tions.[4] This unease is expressed most directly by Robert Solow. In his fore-word, he writes, "Maybe the idea of a unitary decisionmaker—like an optimizing individual or a wise and impartial adviser—is not very helpful when it comes to the choice of policies that will have distant-future effects about which one can now know hardly anything."

There are several reasons for the unease. For one thing, there is no mistaking the very small present value of even very large costs and bene-fits if they will not be realized for hundreds of years. Assume, for exam-ple, that the gross domestic product (GDP) of the world will be $8 quadrillion in the year 2200 in current dollars.[5] Suppose next that we want to calculate the present value of that sum using the 7% discount rate that the Office of Management and Budget recommends for such pur-poses. The answer we get is a surprising $10 *billion*. In other words, it would not make sense for the world's present inhabitants to expend more than $10 billion today (or about $2 per person) on a measure that would prevent the loss of the entire GDP of the world 200 years from now. No matter how familiar one is with the power of compound interest, it is hard not to be stunned by the small difference that the distant future makes for present-day decisionmaking.

The reason that it would not make sense to spend more than $10 bil-lion today to safeguard world GDP 200 years from now is clear, of course. It is that we could invest that same $10 billion at 7% today and have a sum more than sufficient to replace GDP at that time. But this suggests still another concern even hard-nosed benefit-cost analysts have about intertemporal project evaluation: What guarantee is there that the $10 bil-lion, even if set aside in a fund to replace GDP 200 years hence, will be left alone during the intervening years? In other words, what if those populating the earth 100 years from now decide to dip into the fund to finance their own consumption? In such a case, those living 200 years from now will have neither the protection of the project we eschewed today nor the fund we created to make them whole because we rejected that project. The fact that we could make them better off with an alternative investment is of little consolation to them if that investment never reaches maturity.

This leads us to another observation about discounting and intergenerational decisionmaking. Although this is not the case for the contributors to this volume, many of those bothered by discounting what Weitzman (1998) calls the "distant future" or the "far distant future" appear to confuse economic efficiency with distributional equity. That is, they seem to forget that a policy action may be unattractive on distributional grounds even if it passes the efficiency test.

To illustrate, consider a policy change for which all of the benefits and costs will be felt immediately. Even if the benefits exceed the costs by a considerable margin, we might reasonably object to the project. This would be so if, first, all the benefits go to the richest five families in the country while all the costs fall on the poorest five, and second, for institutional or other reasons there is no way to compensate the losers out of the gains to the winners.

The same is true for projects the effects of which are spread out through time. Even if it is efficient to reject a climate protection program, say, because it would be cheaper to invest the money in an interest-bearing asset, one might reasonably object to this decision on distributional grounds, especially if one is dubious that the compensation will actually be available to future generations (see Chapter 2 of this volume). At least some of those uncomfortable with the distributional consequences of climate change seem eager to tinker with the discount rate to make mitigation policies pass the efficiency test (when in fact they may not). There is no need to do so—efficiency is hardly the only criterion that matters in policy analysis.

Another very important point comes out of these chapters—one that goes to the very heart of the questions we posed to the participants in the workshop. *With one exception, every chapter in this volume suggests that it is appropriate—indeed essential—to discount future benefits and costs at some positive rate.* Even the one exception—the chapter by Dasgupta, Mäler, and Barrett, in which they envision circumstances in which the discount rate could be zero or even negative—leaves us with the impression that this would be an unusual case.[6] Even while arguing for a lower discount rate than would be appropriate for a shorter horizon, as many of the chapters here do, the authors quite clearly believe that a failure to discount future benefits and costs would be a recipe for poor intergenerational policy-making. We take this to be one of the most important conclusions a reader might draw from this volume.

We can make an even stronger statement than this, though. At the workshop, during the discussions surrounding the individual papers and particularly during a wide-ranging discussion involving all the partici-pants that followed the last presentation, virtually everyone agreed on a standard procedure for the evaluation of projects with timeframes of forty years or less. Specifically, they agreed not only that it is appropriate to discount benefits and costs for the purposes of making present value comparisons, but also that the discount rate to use should be one that reflects the opportunity cost of capital. In other words, for projects with horizons shorter than forty years, the conferees were squarely in the *descriptive* camp, to use the language of Arrow in the IPCC report. Beyond this horizon, however, discomfort sets in, and the participants were more willing to entertain somewhat different ways to make decisions (see below).

Another theme pops up in several, though not all, of the papers: ana-lysts may want to use different discount rates depending on the period over which they are calculating net present values. Reference is made to this possibility by Arrow (Chapter 2), Weitzman (Chapter 3), and Kopp and Portney (Chapter 9). Moreover, this idea is the central organizing principle in the essay by Cropper and Laibson (Chapter 16). The possibil-ity of nonconstant discounting is suggested by a growing number of stud-ies in which individuals' discount rates are inferred either from their observed behavior in actual markets (Hausman 1979) or their responses to hypothetical questions about their attitudes toward risk (Horowitz 1991), saving behavior (Thaler 1981), or the life-saving activities of gov-ernment (Cropper, Aydede, and Portney 1994).[7] These studies show rather consistently that while individuals do appear to attach lower weights to distant benefits, they not use a constant exponential discount rate. Rather, the longer the time period before effects are felt, the lower the implicit discount rate used.[8]

Finally, and perhaps most surprisingly, at least three of the chapters in this volume explicitly call into question the very utility of the standard welfare-theoretic approach to decisionmaking for climate policy and other problems with significant intergenerational consequences. Schelling, for instance, suggests that we view the problem of climate change in much the same way that we try to decide the right amount of foreign aid to make available to poorer countries each year. His logic is compelling. Most of the costs of mitigating climate change will be borne by the wealthy industrialized countries, while most of the benefits will go to residents of the developing countries, both in the medium and long terms. Thus, as

Schelling sees it, the question is how much will the former sacrifice in the here and now for the benefit of the latter.

Lind is quite sympathetic to Schelling's approach. He compares decisionmaking on climate change to more traditional investment analysis, as in the case of a series of financial options that, once they expire, must be reevaluated (see also Lind and Schuler 1998). While Lind stops short of repudiating the position he set out so elegantly in his 1982 book, for problems like climate change he is clearly wary of policymaking predicated heavily on net present values.

Kopp and Portney take matters one step farther. Sharing Schelling's and Lind's concerns (and perhaps those of other of the participants), they suggest an altogether different approach for decisionmaking in the presence of significant intergenerational effects. Their proposed approach involves a mock referendum, through which is elicited the willingness-to-pay of members of the present generation to reduce the risks to both current and future generations associated with climate change. Aggregate willingness-to-pay (a measure of the current benefits of climate mitigation) would then be compared with the expected costs. This approach would circumvent the need to estimate very long term streams of benefits and costs, as well as the need to choose an appropriate discount rate. Their proposed approach presents formidable problems of its own, however, which would have to compared with those of the more traditional approach.

FINAL THOUGHTS

What accounts, then, for the reemergence of a schism among economists on the appropriate discount rate for projects extending into the far future? For one thing, the "consensus" described above may have been more apparent than real. After all, the energy crisis—which led to the 1977 conference and Lind's subsequent edited volume—began to abate about the time the book came out. This development probably refocused policymakers' attention on much shorter-term issues for which the choice of a discount rate makes little or no difference. Had the energy crisis not abated, Lind's consensus may have proved to be more fragile than we suggested above.

Greater attention is also being paid these days to distributional questions, prompted by the increasing disparity between the incomes of those at the top and those at the bottom of the income scale. It may be natural at such a time to think not only about intra- and international inequalities in income and wealth, but also about the legacy that we may be leaving for future generations. As soon as one begins to consider policies to affect the latter, up pops the issue of discounting.

We suspect, however, that it is the climate change debate that has economists and others thinking hard once again about the treatment of intergenerational benefits and costs. Should this debate recede into the background (an unlikely prospect, we think), disagreements about whether and at what rate to discount may recede with them. But about two things we feel confident: first, there will always be differing views on the appropriateness of discounting, not to mention the rate to use, and second, a careful reading of the essays in this volume will leave readers better prepared to understand what is being debated and why it is important.

ENDNOTES

1. The IPCC is a large group of scientists from around the world that was convened by the World Meteorological Organization and the United Nations Environment Program to study and provide periodic reports on the possible causes and effects of climate change, as well as the consequences of policies designed to mitigate and/or adapt to these effects.

2. Proponents of the descriptive approach bristle—rightfully so, we believe—at the implication that theirs is an "unethical" tack to take. Indeed, they argue, the reason to use a market-based rate when discounting future benefits and costs is to ensure that society invests in those projects, and only those projects, that leave future generations better off than they would otherwise be.

3. Even small differences in discount rates are important, of course. Because of the power of compound interest, a slightly lower rate could mean that many more investment projects (such as measures to mitigate climate change) will be attractive on grounds of economic efficiency.

4. This unease extends well beyond the contributors to this volume; for instance, see also Chichilnisky 1993 and Heal 1997.

5. This is consistent with an annual growth rate of 3% from current world GDP over the next 200 years.

6. The other authors would agree, we believe, that if per capita consumption were expected to *decline* rather than increase over time, one could justify a zero or even negative discount rate. Since all of modern experience is with gradually *increasing* per capita consumption, however, the most reasonable assumption seems to be that future generations will be better off than the present generation. This forms a rationale for a positive discount rate, incidentally, even if we are unwilling to discount because we feel a greater affinity for generations nearer to ours than for those far removed in time.

7. In a recent paper stimulated by and written subsequent to the 1996 conference, Weitzman has provided a rationale for nonconstant discounting. Moreover, using preferences elicited from more than 1,700 economists and a second set of preferences from fifty of those he considers "experts" on discounting, he has derived a schedule showing the discount rate that is appropriate for particular horizons.

8. Using a discount rate that depends on the period over which the analysis is being conducted is not without problems. For one thing, it leads to time-inconsistent decisions: plans that people will not follow if given the opportunity to reconsider their actions. This property of hyperbolic discounting functions makes many people uneasy about their use in benefit-cost analysis.

REFERENCES

Arrow, K. J., W. R. Cline, K.-G. Mäler, M. Munasinghe, R. Squitieri, and J. E. Stiglitz. 1996. Intertemporal Equity, Discounting, and Economic Efficiency. Chapter 4 in J. P. Bruce, H. Lee, and E. F. Haites (eds.), *Climate Change 1995: Economic and Social Dimensions of Climate Change.* Contribution of Working Group III to the Second Assessment Report of the Intergovernmental Panel on Climate Change. Cambridge: Cambridge University Press.

Bradford, David F. 1975. Constraints on Government Investment Opportunities and the Choice of Discount Rate. *American Economic Review* 65(5): 887–99.

Chichilnisky, G. 1993. An Axiomatic Approach to Sustainable Development. *Social Choice and Welfare* 13(2): 219–48

Cropper, M. L., S. K. Aydede, and P. R. Portney. 1994. Preferences for Life-Saving Programs: How the Public Discounts Time and Age. *Journal of Risk and Uncertainty* 8(3): 243–46.

Diamond, P. 1968. The Opportunity Cost of Public Investment: Comment. *Quarterly Journal of Economics* 686–88.

Eckstein, O. 1958. *Water Resource Development: The Economics of Project Evaluation.* Cambridge, Massachusetts: Harvard University Press.

Feldstein, M. 1970. Financing in the Evaluation of Public Expenditure. Discussion Paper No. 132, Harvard Institute for Economic Research.

Hausman, Jerry A. 1979. Individual Discount Rates and the Purchase and Utilization of Energy-Using Durables. *The Bell Journal of Economics* 10: 33–54.

Heal, G. 1997. Valuing Our Future: Cost-Benefit Analysis and Sustainability. Discussion Paper No. 13, United Nations Development Program, Office of Development Studies.

Horowitz, J. 1991. Discounting Monetary Payoffs: An Experimental Analysis. In *Handbook of Behavioral Economics,* edited by S. Kaish and B. Gilad. Greenwich, Connecticut: JAI Press.

IPCC (Intergovernmental Panel on Climate Change). 1996. *Climate Change 1995: Economic and Social Dimensions of Climate Change.* Contribution of Working Group III to the Second Assessment Report of the IPCC. Cambridge: Cambridge University Press.

Lind, Robert C., ed. 1982. *Discounting for Time and Risk in Energy Policy.* Baltimore: Johns Hopkins University Press for Resources for the Future.

Lind, R. C., and R. Schuler. 1998. Equity and Discounting in Climate-Change Decisions. In *Economics and Policy Issues in Climate Change,* edited by W. Nordhaus. Washington, D.C.: Resources for the Future.

Morgenstern, Richard, ed. 1997. *Economic Analyses at EPA: Assessing Regulatory Impact.* Washington, D.C.: Resources for the Future.

Thaler, Richard. 1981. Some Empirical Evidence on Dynamic Inconsistency. *Economic Letters* 8: 201–7.

Weitzman, M. 1998. Gamma Discounting for Global Warming. Discussion Paper, Harvard University, Department of Economics.

2

Discounting, Morality, and Gaming

Kenneth J. Arrow

I take the problem of discounting for projects with payoffs in the far future (climate change, nuclear waste disposal) to be largely ethical. There is an apparent conflict in our moral intuitions, already apparent in Ramsey's work (1928). On the one hand, moral considerations are based on universalizability, in which case we should treat future generations as we would ourselves, so that the pure rate of pure time preference should be zero. But with zero time preference and a long horizon, the savings rates become inordinately high, possibly approaching one as the horizon goes to infinity (Koopmans 1960). A reconciliation must be based on the notion that individuals are not morally required to subscribe fully to morality at any cost to themselves. There are both empirical evidence and theoretical arguments that individuals recognize moral arguments for the far future but treat themselves and the near future better (Chichilnisky 1996; Cropper, Aydede, and Portney 1994). This approach leads to a non-cooperative game, in which each generation is somewhat selfish (compared with perfect morality) and recognizes that future generations will be similarly selfish. I thus come back to the very original paper of Phelps and Pollak (1968). Whether this point of view leads to discounting long-lived irreversible investments at a lower rate than short-term investments depends on circumstances. But, I believe it typically does not.

THE DILEMMA OF EQUAL TREATMENT

Starting, as I have, with an ethical viewpoint, the problem is, how can people be treated differently just because they are at different places in

KENNETH J. ARROW, 1972 Nobel Laureate in economics, is presently Joan Kenney Professor of Economics Emeritus at Stanford University.

13

time. The English economists tended to be very scornful of pure time preference. Pigou (1932, 25) stated rather politely that pure time preference "implies ... our telescopic faculty is defective." Ramsey and Harrod were more morally assertive. Ramsey (1928, 261): "[I]t is assumed that we do not discount later enjoyments in comparison with earlier ones, a practice which is ethically indefensible and arises merely from the weakness of the imagination." Harrod (1948, 40): "[P]ure time preference [is] a polite expression for rapacity and the conquest of reason by passion."

Koopmans, who has, in fact, given the basic argument *for* discounting, nevertheless holds "an ethical preference for neutrality as between the welfare of different generations" (1965, 239). Robert Solow (1974, 9): "In solemn conclave assembled, so to speak, we ought to act as if the social rate of time preference were zero." When the conclave is not so solemn, different thoughts appear. Ramsey presented a talk to a group of friends at Cambridge (the Society, frequently referred to as the Apostles), in which, talking about our observations of the universe, he said, "My picture of the world is drawn in perspective.... I apply my perspective not merely to space but also to time. In time the world will cool and everything will die; but that is a long way off still, and *its present value at compound interest is almost nothing*" (Ramsey 1931, 291; emphasis added).

Why then not embrace the idea of zero time perspective? Koopmans, in several classic papers (1960, 1965), gave a crushing answer; see also Brown and Lewis (1981) for a more general treatment. The argument seems recondite. Koopmans considers a world that lasts forever. Therefore, choice (including ethically based choice) is based on a preference ordering over infinite-dimensional consumption streams. He argues that if the ordering is continuous and also sensitive (that is, if one stream is never worse than another and is better at one or more time points, then it must be strictly preferred), it must display impatience.

A simple restatement of his reasoning can bring out the essential point. I confine myself to the intertemporally separable case. Imagine initially that output consists of a constant stream of completely perishable goods. There can be no investment by definition. Now imagine that an investment opportunity occurs, available only to the first generation. For each unit sacrificed by them, a perpetual stream of α per unit time is generated. If there were no time preference, what would the optimal solution be? Each unit sacrificed would yield a finite utility loss to the first generation, but to compensate, there would be a gain, however small, to each of an infinity of generations. Thus, *any* sacrifice by the first generation is good. Strictly speaking, we cannot say that the first generation should sacrifice everything, if marginal utility approaches infinity as consumption approaches zero. But, we can say that given any investment, short of the entire income, a still greater investment would be preferred.

I think it is fair to say that this implication is unacceptable. We can generalize. Not merely is saving arbitrarily close to 100% unacceptable, but very high sacrifices are also. I call this the *weak Koopmans argument*. This will meet a possible objection to the argument of the last paragraph. The proposed investment opportunity set is, indeed, very artificial. If the investment is feasible today, it should also be feasible in all future periods. From the perspective of the logic of choice, this is not a valid objection. If a preference ordering is suitable and meaningful, then it should explain behavior under any physically possible opportunity set, not merely "realistic" ones. In the usual theory of choice that serves as a basis for competitive equilibrium theory, we assume choices possible between any pairs of alternatives, although in the application, we see only choices within budget sets.

But, let me waive this defense. Suppose, in fact, that the investment opportunity described is available in every period. This is the standard pure capital model. To get a definite result, assume that utility is intertemporally additive and that the felicity function (utility in any one period) is a power function.

$$U(c_t) = \frac{c_t^{1-\theta}}{(1-\theta)}, \theta > 1 \tag{1}$$

In the absence of pure time preference, the maximand is

$$W = \Sigma U(c_t) \tag{2}$$

(The assumption $\theta > 1$ implies an upper bound to U and therefore permits, in suitable cases, the existence of an optimum.) Under the assumptions made, the opportunity sets for each period are, of course, characterized by the difference equation,

$$K_{t+1} = \alpha(K_t - c_t) \tag{3}$$

where K_t is capital or accumulated savings at time t, and K_0 is given. The continuous-time version of this case was already analyzed in Ramsey's original paper (1928, 276), and he showed that the optimal savings ratio (that is, ratio of savings to *income*) is $1/\theta$ (independent of the productivity α).

Reasonable estimates of θ are, of course, hard to come by, but there have been a few attempts (see Intergovernmental Panel on Climate Change chapter on discounting, cited as Arrow and others [1996, 236]). They find that θ is 1.5 or less. If this is so, then the implied savings rate is two-thirds or more.

I find this to be an incredible and unacceptable strain on the present generation. Even Ramsey (1928, 278) remarks, after calculating savings ratios in a pure capital model for several plausible values of the elasticity of the marginal utility, θ: "The rate of saving which the rule requires is greatly in excess of that which anyone would normally suggest."

I, therefore, conclude that the strong ethical requirement that all generations be treated alike, itself reasonable, contradicts a very strong intuition that it is not morally acceptable to demand excessively high savings rates of any one generation, or even of every generation.

AGENT-RELATIVE ETHICS

I do not think this dilemma arises merely out of the specifically utilitarian formulation that welfare economists find so congenial. It is a conflict between a basic principle of morality, as seen by many philosophers and others, that of *universalizability*, and a principle of self-regard, of the individual as an end and not merely a means to the welfare of others. In a favorite quotation of mine, Hillel, the first-century rabbi, asked, "If I am not for myself, then who is for me? If I am not for others, then who am I? If not now, when?" One can only say that *both* the universal other and the self impose obligations on an agent.

After coming to the conclusion that it is not necessarily obligatory to fully comply with impersonally moral obligation, I found, not surprisingly, that this point has been made by others, most especially the philosopher Samuel Scheffler (1982; revised edition 1994); see also the anthology of writings on this issue edited by Scheffler (1988).[1] The same point has been suggested in passing by the economist Yew-Kwang Ng (1989, 243). In fact, I had a model of intragenerational income redistribution in which the welfare of each individual was the utility of private consumption plus the sum of all other private utilities, the utilities for each individual being scaled so that at a given income level, the marginal utility for self was higher than that for others (Arrow 1981). "Morality" here consisted of treating everyone else equally, and there was, indeed, a trade-off between individual welfare and moral obligation.

In the intergenerational context, it is important to note that the agent in each generation is that generation, not the set of all generations beginning with that one. Hence, agent-relative ethics suggests that each generation will maximize a weighted sum of its own utility and the sum of utilities of all future generations, with less weight on the latter. At the very least, really distant generations are treated all alike. Now, this is precisely the outcome of the questionnaire study of Cropper, Aydede, and Portney (1994); respondents weighted returns one hundred years from now, although exponential discounting would lead to a very different outcome. From a theoretical perspective, Chichilnisky (1996) has given a plausible set of axioms on individual attitudes to the future that lead to results similar to those of Cropper, Aydede, and Portney.

However, this is not the end of the story. It gives a way of understanding the welfare function of any one generation. But no one generation controls the future. Each generation can determine how it will divide its disposable income among consumption and various kinds of investments, public or private. But the next generation will have the same decision. If all investment is short-lived (or, more generally, reversible), then all that one generation can determine is how much capital to pass on to its immediate successor. That generation, in turn, will decide what it will leave to the next, and so forth.

Hence, what one generation leaves will be influenced by its expectation of what the next generation will do with its income, which is wholly or partly determined by what the first generation gives it. The second-generation allocation (as a function of the capital it receives) will determine the utility of the first generation's bequest to the latter and therefore determine (in part) the amount the first generation will leave.

This becomes a game among the successive generations, which has already been analyzed in a classic paper by Phelps and Pollak (1968).[2] I will not analyze the details of the solution here, though I believe they have very interesting implications for setting discount rates. But there is one point that emerges clearly. The future, looked at from each point, looks the same, except possibly for a different initial capital stock. Then, the actual equilibrium path is more or less what it would be with some particular discount rate; at least this is true if the felicity functions are power functions. Even though no individual discounts the future exponentially, the equilibrium path will be that corresponding to an exponentially discounted path.

IRREVERSIBLE INVESTMENT

The present generation, in its desire for impartiality among its successors, may be appalled at the selfishness of the next generation and try to overcome its consequences. Can it do anything? Yes, there are many real investments that yield benefits to the distant future and that either cannot be plundered by the intervening generations or will yield relatively little if they do try to interfere. A giant dam, such as Hoover Dam in Nevada, could be destroyed to recover the concrete and piping, but it would hardly pay. Instead, a benefit in the form of controlled water flow is available for at least a century, guaranteed to the future. Similarly, some of the proposals for nuclear waste disposal involve commitments to the very distant future.

But elementary theory shows that irreversible investment has very little power to control the future. Indeed, so long as there is in each generation a certain amount of additional investment, there can be essentially no control at all by a generation beyond its immediate successor. For in that case, the marginal investment is controlled by the intermediate generation. If Generation 1 makes provision for Generation 3 by means of a long-term irreversible investment, more than Generation 2 would have done, Generation 2 will simply reduce its investments by a corresponding amount. Only if Generation 2 will leave nothing can Generation 1's intentions be carried out.

(To be sure, it is possible that an early generation can control the *direction* of investment, though not the amount. Thus, a generation devoted to water resource development can supply more than the next generation would like. The latter might be able to adjust only by investments in other directions, such as private goods. But, if we are interested in total welfare, this qualification is not significant.)

Let me conclude with a simple example. There are three generations, labeled unimaginatively 1, 2, and 3. The felicity of each generation is logarithmic,

$$U(c_t) = \ln c_t \ (t = 1, 2, 3)$$

Generation 1 has one unit of income; there are no given incomes for Generations 2 and 3. Generation 1 has two possible investments. Investment 1 lasts one period and yields α_1 per unit invested. Investment 2 yields no return in the first subsequent period and α_2 in the second period. Generation 2 has the same options, but, of course, it will not invest in Investment 2, since the world ends with Generation 3.

In accordance with the preceding discussion, Generation 1 wants to maximize

$$\ln c_1 + \delta(\ln c_2 + \ln c_3) \tag{4}$$

If it invests K^1_i in Investment I ($I = 1, 2$), consider the decision of Generation 2, whose maximand is

$$\ln c_2 + \delta \ln c_3$$

Generation 3 is already receiving an income $\alpha_2 K^1_2$. Let K^2_1 be the investment of Generation 2 in Investment 1. By definition,

$$c_2 + K^2_{\ 1} = \alpha_1 K^1_{\ 1}$$

$$c_3 = \alpha_1 K^2_{\ 1} + \alpha_2 K^1_{\ 2}$$

Eliminate $K^2_{\ 1}$ between these equations.

$$c_2 + \alpha_1^{-1} c_3 = \alpha_1^{-1}\alpha_2 K^1_{\ 2} + \alpha_1 K^1_{\ 1} \tag{5}$$

If we maximize equation (4) subject to equation (5), we see that c_2 and c_3 are increasing functions of the right-hand side of equation (5). Hence, Generation 1 wants to maximize that expression, subject to the constraint

$$c_1 + K^1_{\ 1} + K^1_{\ 2} = 1$$

Hence, for any given c_1, Generation 1 wants to maximize the right-hand side of equation (5) subject to a constant value of $K^1_{\ 1} + K^1_{\ 2}$. Clearly, this means that if the long-term investment has a lower rate of return, it is not used. That is, if

$$\alpha_1^{\ 2} > \alpha_2 \tag{6}$$

then the long-term investment will not be made.

Now this analysis, however, ignored the possibility that generation's choice of $K^2_{\ 1}$ might be negative, which is impossible. That is, $K^1_{\ 2}$ might be so large that Generation 2 will be at a boundary and will leave nothing to Generation 3, in which case the foregoing formulas are invalid. The fuller statement is that if equation (6) holds, then there are two possible strategies for Generation 1; either it makes both kinds of investment with the understanding that Generation 2 will leave nothing to Generation 3, or it makes only the short-term investment and relies on Generation 2's concern for Generation 3.

By elementary calculations in the foregoing model, it can be shown that if

$$\frac{\alpha_2 > 4\delta\alpha_1^{\ 2}}{(1+\delta)^2}$$

then Generation 1 will find it best to determine future consumption by its allocation between the two kinds of investment, under the assumption that Generation 2 will not make any provision for Generation 3, while in the reverse case, the best strategy for Generation 1 is to make only the more productive short-term investment.

It seems to me that the typical situation is that there is a large variety of short-term or reversible investments and these determine the margin. It follows that ordinarily there is no argument for discounting irreversible investments at a lower rate, in spite of the evidence that this is what each generation would prefer.

ENDNOTES

[1]I am indebted to Derek Parfit for the references to Scheffler's work.

[2]Dasgupta (1974) has developed a similar game interpretation to develop a theory of just savings along Rawlsian lines.

REFERENCES

Arrow, K. J. 1981. Optimal and Voluntary Income Distribution. In S. Rosefielde (ed.), *Economic Welfare and the Economics of Soviet Socialism: Essays in Honor of Abram Bergson*. Cambridge: Cambridge University Press, 267–88.

Arrow, K. J., W. R. Cline, K.-G. Mäler, M. Munasinghe, R. Squitieri, and J. E. Stiglitz. 1996. Intertemporal Equity, Discounting, and Economic Efficiency. In J. P. Bruce, H. Lee, and E. F. Haites (eds.), *Climate Change 1995: Economic and Social Dimensions of Climate Change*. Contribution of Working Group III to the Second Assessment Report of the Intergovernmental Panel on Climate Change. Cambridge: Cambridge University Press.

Brown, D. G., and L. Lewis. 1981. Myopic Economic Agents. *Econometrics* 49(2): 359–68.

Chichilnisky, G. 1996. An Axiomatic Approach to Sustainable Development. *Social Choice and Welfare* 13: 231–57.

Cropper, M., S. K. Aydede, and P. R. Portney. 1994. Preferences for Life Saving Programs: How the Public Discounts Time and Age. *Journal of Risk and Uncertainty* 8(3): 243–46.

Dasgupta, P. 1974. On Some Problems Arising from Professor Rawls's Conception of Distributive Justice. *Theory and Decision* 4: 325–44.

Harrod, R. F. 1948. *Towards a Dynamic Economics*. London: Macmillan.

Koopmans, T. C. 1960. Stationary Ordinal Utility and Impatience. *Econometrica* 28: 287–309.

———. 1965. On the Concept of Optimal Economic Growth. In *The Econometric Approach to Development Planning*. Amsterdam: North Holland, and Chicago: Rand McNally, 225–87.

Ng, Y.-K. 1989. What Should We Do About Future Generations? Impossibility of Parfit's Theory X. *Economics and Philosophy* 5: 235–53.

Phelps, E. S., and R. Pollak. 1968. On Second-Best National Saving and Game–Equilibrium Growth. *Review of Economic Studies* 35(2): 185–99.

Pigou, A. C. 1932. *The Economics of Welfare*. 4th ed. London: Macmillan.

Ramsey, F. P. 1928. A Mathematical Theory of Saving. *Economic Journal* 38: 543–49. Reprinted in F. P. Ramsey. *Foundations: Essays in Philosophy, Logic, Mathematics, and Economics*. Edited by D. H. Mellor. 261–81. (Page references in text are for the reprint.)

———. 1931. *The Foundations of Mathematics and Other Logical Essays*. London: Routledge and Kegan Paul.

Scheffler, S. 1982. *The Rejection of Consequentialism*. Oxford and New York: Clarendon Press. Revised edition, 1994.

———, ed. 1988. *Consequentialism and Its Critics*. Oxford and New York: Oxford University Press.

Schelling, T. C. 1995. Intergenerational Discounting. *Energy Policy* 23 (4–5): 395–401.

Solow, R. 1974. The Economics of Resources or the Resources of Economics. *American Economic Review Papers and Proceedings* 64 (2).

3

"Just Keep Discounting, But..."

Martin L. Weitzman

We at this workshop have been asked to address a seemingly arcane issue of technical economics that has important real-world consequences. Furthermore, we have been asked to explain this issue, and to explain how we think it should be resolved, in a language and a style that can be understood by an interested general audience.

The seemingly arcane issue concerns how to discount events that come to pass in what I shall call the "deep future"—meaning they will happen many generations, even centuries, from now, long after we and everyone we know have passed away. At first thought it might seem that such projects are of limited practical importance. Maybe that was true once, but increasingly today we are being asked to analyze projects whose effects will be spread out over hundreds of years. The most prominent single example of this is the mother of environmental catastrophes—global warming. Examples other than global climate change include: radioactive waste disposal, biodiversity loss, stratospheric ozone, groundwater pollution, and mineral depletion. Projects or activities with prominent deep-future payoffs are all over the environmental landscape today.

Now, a funny thing happened to us economists on the way to the forum when we tried to apply standard benefit-cost methods to these really long-term effects. It turned out that the deep-future part of deep-future projects didn't much matter. For any reasonable discount rates (above a couple or so percentage points per year), what happens a few centuries from now hardly counts at all. The reason, as I am sure most people here know, is the extraordinary power of compound interest to discount a deep-future dollar's worth of goods and services into near nothingness as measured by today's dollars.

MARTIN L. WEITZMAN is the Ernest E. Monrad Professor of Economics at Harvard University.

What this result means is something like the following. Global warming might cause a rise in sea level, which in turn could cause flooding in low-lying cities if they were not walled off and pumped out. But if and when this event happens two centuries or more into the future, it's not such a big deal because a very modest savings program started now would accumulate enough bricks and metal and so forth that we could easily afford to build the walls and pumps and everything else we would need *if the underlying trend of the real rate of interest remains about the same.* This, I believe, is the key issue in deep-future discounting, and we should not be led astray by the numerous sideshows that impair focusing directly on it.

The remainder of the paper, then, tries to answer the key question: what is our best prediction of the real rate of interest into the deep future?

Well, what drives deep-future real interest rates? For that matter, what determines the underlying trend of the real rate of interest more generally?

For society as a whole, our economy acts like one big bank account. If we decide to curtail our consumption this year by saving an extra dollar's worth of consumption, that's just like depositing an extra dollar's worth of the underlying resources, which have been liberated by our refraining from consuming them, into society's big bank account to be recycled for capital formation. The amount of extra future output that we get from such an act of saving is, essentially, the real interest rate. The value of the real interest rate is just the return on the loans that the bank can make with our savings, otherwise known as the "productivity of investment."

So, the real rate of interest for any time period is determined by the productivity of investment in that period. What drives the deep-future interest rate is then the same force or forces that drive the deep-future productivity of investment.

What the economists on their way to the forum are doing when they apply standard benefit-cost methodology to deep-future projects is something like the following. They assume, implicitly, that the productivity of investment in the deep future will be about the same as it has been in the recent past. Since it is a fair generalization to say that the rate of return on capital has been essentially trendless over past periods for which we have data, it seems like a reasonable procedure to project this trendless real interest rate forward to the deep future. Or is it so reasonable?

An old debate on the so-called "limits to growth"—defined broadly—has been taking place for a long time now. Although the exact content of the debate may differ from decade to decade, its generic form is surprisingly invariant over several centuries.

The "growth pessimist" has a world view of history wherein humanity is condemned to be navigating toward a horizon over which looms stagnation, or worse, because we will run out of one limiting factor or another—like land, labor, minerals, a clean environment, or whatever. Then diminishing returns will set in, choking off growth.

"Diminishing returns" in this context means that the productivity of investment declines to zero in the deep future because so much capital will have been accumulated by then that more of it is no longer effective in substituting for the limiting factor or factors.

By contrast, the typical economist tends to be a "growth optimist," believing that human ingenuity will always rescue the day because, in the words of J. M. Clark, "knowledge is the only instrument of production not subject to diminishing returns."

Thus, the "limits to growth" debate is in essence a debate about the deep-future productivity of capital. Which side is right?

The forces that determine the deep-future productivity of capital are essentially the same forces that determine deep-future productivity more generally. Productivity is just output per unit of inputs.

It turns out that a long line of extremely important economic research has proven beyond any reasonable doubt that, almost no matter how it is measured, long-term productivity has grown over time at a more or less trendless rate. Whether we look at time series of raw tons of outputs over raw tons of inputs, or quality-adjusted tons of outputs over quality-adjusted tons of inputs, or dollars-worth of outputs over dollars-worth of inputs, or almost-anything-weighted outputs over almost-anything-weighted inputs, the ratio just seems to keep growing trendlessly over time.

The reason that we keep on getting ever more units of output per unit of inputs is because of "technical progress," which is just a synonym for human ingenuity or inventiveness. It is technical progress that, by warding off diminishing returns, prevents capital productivity from falling over time. Like a magic cook in a fairy tale, we seem always to be able to conjure up fantastic new recipes for combining inputs to make bigger portions of food out of the same base of raw ingredients.

The chain of reasoning looks like this so far. Deep-future interest rates are driven by essentially the same forces that drive deep-future capital productivity, which is driven by essentially the same forces that motivate and propel human inventiveness in conjuring up new ways to offset diminishing returns. So a projection of real interest rates from the recent past into the deep future is very much the same thing as an extrapolation of the rate of technical change from the recent past into the deep future. Everything, then, comes down to estimating the deep-future effectiveness of human ingenuity to come up with new recipes of production for new circumstances.

Is it possible to conceive of a world where we run out of productive new ideas? Yes, in a way it is. All inventors have times when they just don't seem able to think up creative new ideas, or the potentially new ideas just don't seem to work out. All of us academic researchers have had dry spells where we go through the motions of research, we continue the finger exercises, but we don't really have any good ideas and can't come up with anything truly original. As it is for individuals, so it is for companies, or sectors of an economy, or even whole societies. It seems that some periods are just not very fruitful for human ingenuity or inventiveness. At a very high level of abstraction, then, it is possible to imagine a time of no technical progress because there just happens to have been a streak of bad luck during that time.

But is it possible to imagine a deep-future world in which the state of knowledge is perpetually stagnant? After all, maybe good ideas are like stars in the sky—there are a lot of them out there to be discovered but not an infinite number, and eventually even the stars run out. It might feel very frustrating to live in such a twilight world of no technical progress, where we would be having always the empty sensation that anything we could invent has already been invented. But there is no reason in principle why God made the universe with an infinite supply of good ideas. Or is there?

If your intuition is like mine, something will strike you as intrinsically implausible about a world supposedly in a steady state where it is impossible to think up any fruitful new inventions. In a world like this, the production of new knowledge would be a process akin to the discovery of new oil fields, where even the cleverest geologist some day finds that there is just no more oil to be discovered.

It seems to me that something fundamentally different is involved here. When research effort is applied, new ideas arise out of existing ideas in some kind of cumulative interactive process that intuitively has a very different feel from prospecting for petroleum. To me, the research process has a sort of pattern-fitting or combinatoric feel about it. It seems that ideas build upon each other in such a way that many new ideas are essentially successful reconfigurations of already existing ideas that have not previously been combined with each other. If it is true that many basic ideas can be viewed as combinations of other basic ideas, then there is the potential for knowledge to build upon itself by a kind of self-generating recombinant feedback process where the discovery of new ideas itself generates further new ideas by combinations of the new with the old.

The power of combinatorics becomes overwhelming past a certain point. Most people do not appreciate the fantastically large number of ways that even familiar everyday objects like cards in a deck or bits on a hard-disk drive can be combined with each other. It has been calculated that the number of different bit strings that can be put on today's average personal computer disk is larger than the number of elementary particles in the universe, while the number of ways to arrange an ordinary deck of playing cards exceeds the number of seconds that have elapsed since the big bang. Imagine, then, what eventually happens to a dynamic process where the number of playing cards in the deck is itself an endogenously determined variable that increases in proportion to the number of untried card arrangements. A growth process whose increments are based on any positive fraction of previously untried combinations may start out growing very slowly. But even for the tiniest proportionality factor, given enough time a combinatoric growth process will always end up overwhelming any growth process based on mere geometric expansion.

If this way of looking at the world is correct, and ideas are fundamentally self generating, I don't think we are going to run out of new inventions. The germ of truth here, which I think is relatively robust, is that if we buy into the idea of combinatoric innovation augmenting a fixed factor, then there is a sense in which we have to bend over backwards *not* to buy into the undoing of diminishing returns as an ultimate retardant of economic growth. If the essence of the creative act consists of cleverly combining and recombining useful existing ideas to fashion useful new ideas, then there is truly a rigorous sense in which human ingenuity can be said to have the potential to overcome diminishing returns.

Coming back to the main strand, I don't see fundamental reasons, or what might be called "reasons of principle," why the productivity of capital in the deep future should be lower than it is today. And following that observation, I don't see fundamental reasons why we should not keep on discounting the deep future at today's best estimates of the rate of return to capital. After all, the very nature of deep-future projects allows us to revisit them after five or ten years with new information, including updated discount rates, if we think something has changed.

It is true that elements of "irreversibility" may be involved—both on the side of environmental damages and on the side of investments to offset those damages. An argument based on "irreversibility" per se can be made to cut either way on the issue of slowing down or speeding up remedial action. If our best benefit-cost analysis is indicating strongly that no action is warranted, then I guess I think our best general response is to do nothing now and revisit the issue in five years. So I guess my advice in this case would be the deep-future equivalent of: "take an aspirin now and call me in the morning."

Incidentally, for the purposes of the present paper I think it is largely beside the point to get enmeshed in a detailed discussion about which interest rate out there in the real world is most appropriate to employ as a starting point for benefit-cost analysis, and I sidestep this aspect here. Unless one is prepared to argue the extraordinarily radical proposition that the relevant discount rate should be "adjusted" almost to zero, the fundamental issues raised by deep-future discounting are not pertinently affected by whether this or that real-world interest rate is being used as an initial approximation in benefit-cost calculations.

Why, then, all this controversy, all this fuss and angst, about deep-future discounting? I'm not really sure, but I think that some of it might have to do with the paradoxical nature of compound interest itself. If the power of compound interest over decades or generations is counterintuitive, then perhaps deep-future compounding represents the ultimate paradox of this type.

Suppose you were to sit a schoolchild down in front of a chess board, lay a penny on the first square, two pennies on the second square, four on the third, eight on the fourth, and then ask what would eventually happen if you were to keep on playing this game of "Doubling the Pennies." The answer is that by the time you get to the sixty-fourth square, the value of the pennies would exceed the total wealth of everything in the world. A youngster will have no comprehension of what this means. Why? Because the long term power of compound interest is very counterintuitive!

The deep-future power of compound interest is the ultimate paradox of this genre. It really looks as if it would not make much difference in the relevant units of today's standard of living whether climate change from global warming comes 200 years from now or 400 years from now.

Up to now, this paper is exactly (word-for-word) the paper that I wrote for the conference in November of 1996. The paper to this point represents what I thought *then*. But something happened since then. The conference itself gave me a motivation and an excuse to reflect upon deep-future discounting. As is evident by the text to this point, it was pretty clear to me that the deep-future productivity of capital is actually highly uncertain. When I got to thinking further about it, something started gnawing at me about the peculiar way in which uncertain interest rates need to be averaged over time, and how that might conceivably force a revision in how we conceptualize the problem for the very long run. Then, about a year after the conference was held, the light bulb that signals the "Eureka" experience finally flashed on in my head. (The details are spelled out in a technical working paper entitled "Why the Far-Distant Future Should Be Discounted at its Lowest Possible Rate," available on request.)

The *But...* part of the present paper's title is this: While there is uncertainty about almost everything in the deep future, perhaps the most fundamental uncertainty of all concerns the discount rate itself. As seen from today, the deep-future interest rate is a true random variable for all of the reasons that make the far-distant productivity of capital uncertain. Well, so what? Why not just take expected or average values of interest rates, like we always do? Here is why not!

The variable that should be probability-averaged over various uncertain states of the world is not discount *rates* like r, but discount *factors* like $1/(1 + r)^t$. And this can make an incredible difference for the deep future, when t is very large. In the limit, the properly averaged certainty-equivalent discount *factor* corresponds to the *minimum* discount *rate* having any positive probability mass. From today's perspective, the only relevant limiting scenario is the one with the lowest interest rate—all of the other states at that far-distant time, by comparison, are relatively much less important now because their expected present value is so severely shrunk by the power of compound interest at a higher rate.

What does this mean for the optimal form of a deep-future project like ameliorating the impact of global warming? In effect, the basic idea should make itself felt by biasing strongly the choice of policy instruments and levels of imposed stringency *as if* toward what is optimal for the low-interest-rate scenario, because that scenario will weigh most heavily in the expected difference between benefits and costs.

Uncertainty about future interest rates provides a strong generic rationale for using certainty-equivalent social interest rates that decline over time from around today's observable market values down to the smallest imaginable rates for the far-distant future. As a policy matter, this effect does not "kick in" until we are out of the range of a near-future period within which we can feel confident projecting forward today's relevant interest rates. However, for deep-future projects the effect of declining interest rates might be very important.

Playing casually with some numerical examples suggests to me a sliding-scale social discounting strategy something like the following. For about the next 25 years from the present, use a "low-normal" real annual interest rate of around 3–4%. For the period from about 25 to about 75 years from the present, use a within-period instantaneous interest rate of around 2%. For the period from about 75 to about 300 years from the present, use a within-period instantaneous interest rate of around 1%. And for more than about 300 years from the present, use a within-period instantaneous interest rate of around 0%.

So, I now think the moral of the story is "just keep discounting, but..." at a declining interest rate for very long-term projects.

4

Reconciling Philosophy and Economics in Long-Term Discounting

Comments on Arrow and Weitzman

Michael A. Toman

The chapters by Professors Weitzman and Arrow provide excellent summaries of two complementary arguments for long-term discounting. Weitzman argues that resources should be allocated to maximize their value independently of how they are distributed. In the context Weitzman considers, one does future generations no favors by making intergenerational investments in environmental protection whose yield is lower than the long-term rate of return to capital, which in turn is critically influenced by long-term trends in productivity improvement. He thus rejects the notion that we should tamper with the intertemporal allocation of capital by using "special" discount rates to allocate government expenditure for environmental protection or to justify government regulation.

Weitzman does conclude that in practice the discount rate used to evaluate long-term impacts should be lower than the rate applied to shorter-term impacts. There is uncertainty about future returns to capital which has asymmetric impacts on the present value of future benefits and costs. If the future rate of return to capital is high, then environmental impacts on the long-term future will be even less important; but if the

MICHAEL A. TOMAN is Senior Fellow and Director of the Energy and Natural Resources Division at Resources for the Future.

realized return on capital turns out to be low, then future impacts could be much more important. It is important to note that Weitzman's argument refers *only* to the calculation of a time path of discount rates for certainty-equivalent analysis. The argument does *not* depend on the notion that preferences are, or should be, time-inconsistent, for example.

Professor Arrow focuses more directly on intergenerational welfare allocation. The core of his argument is the point made by Koopmans and others (in economics and philosophy) that there is a tension between concern for the future and concern for ourselves. In particular, a zero or near-zero rate of social time preference implies an implausibly high willingness to defer one's own consumption to save for future generations. Nor can the current generation compel its immediate successor to share its own high-minded concern for the future, since a more rapacious future generation simply would undo a high current savings rate with a low rate of its own. From these observations, Arrow concludes that a positive and constant exponential discount rate is appropriate for evaluating intergenerational investments and impacts, even in the face of irreversible investment.

What conclusions can one draw from these two papers for the practical application of discounting in evaluating future impacts, investments, or policies? The papers do not resolve the long-standing debate among economists and others over the extent to which discount rates should reflect the rate of return on capital or individuals' rates of time preference, let alone the numerical specification of discount rates. Arrow's paper emphasizes considerations related to preferences, while Weitzman's paper emphasizes the rate of return to capital.

A more fundamental consideration is how the problem of intergenerational discounting should be defined. I think that Schelling (1995) and Howarth (1996) make a compelling argument that problems of intergenerational distribution are fundamentally different from problems of present value maximization within one generation (though the implications they draw for climate change risks and policy differ). At issue in intergenerational resource allocation is the willingness of members of the current generation to pay for actions that reduce risks faced by future generations, not the impatience of members of the current generation per se. Arrow's analysis touches on this issue of concern for future generations, but it does not fully develop the implications of this interdependence.

While Weitzman does not directly address the issue, he does argue that there is little need for concern about intergenerational distribution. Based on experience to date, Weitzman asserts, there appears to be no reason to assume that long-term productivity growth will slow—indeed, "combinatorial synergies" in inventions could cause the rate of innovation to accelerate and thereby overcome even geometric growth in real

resource costs from depletion of natural resources (this is a more sophisticated version of the hypothesis in Stiglitz 1974. Weitzman acknowledges
that irreversible harms may arise from the actions of the current generation, but he asserts that irreversibilities could just as easily favor less versus more current remedial action to reduce long-term risks (in order to
avoid premature sunk costs, a point developed by Kolstad 1996). For
example, greenhouse gas emissions may force future generations to
spend more on protecting themselves from adverse effects of climate
change, but Weitzman posits that they would still be better off at the margin if we burn fossil energy and make high-yield capital investments than
if we make protective investments with a lower rate of return.

While Weitzman's thesis probably is widely (but not universally)
shared among economists, other experts would disagree (as illustrated by
debates over the risks of climate change). Ultimately, the issue turns on
empirical questions about the rate of return on alternative investments
that will be debated for some time to come. We can note, however, that to
the extent that the marginal cost of reducing future risks rises over time,
the implications for evaluating policies are similar to the use of a lower
discount rate (though the conceptually correct way to address these factors is in the evaluation of the benefit and cost streams rather than
through modifying the discount rate).[1] This provides another argument
in principle, along with Weitzman's certainty-equivalent analysis, for less
heavily discounting long-term impacts.

As Kopp and Portney argue in this volume (see Chapter 9), empirical
understanding of the willingness of members of the current generation to
sacrifice some of their own consumption opportunities to reduce environmental risks faced by future generations is very limited. There is no reason to believe that this willingness to pay is constant across types or scales
of risks faced by future generations. Kneese and Schultz (1985) echo Ramsey (1928) in suggesting that rendering threats to the more distant future
trivial by discounting seems to offend moral sensibilities. A richer specification of agents' preference orderings over income distributions and ecological risks might be useful to capture aversion to different types of risks.
For example, concern for the future may be less sensitive to the timing of
a risk if that risk is seen to involve some large threshold effect on the
long-term well-being of many future generations.

However one assesses the importance of reducing intergenerational
environmental risks, the costs of risk reduction should be realistically estimated using whatever discount rate approach one deems appropriate for
calculating opportunity costs. This point (made in the general discussion
at the workshop by David Montgomery) responds in part to Professor
Weitzman's concern about favoring certain activities in a way that distorts
the overall allocation of investment. The assessment of the benefits of

action, on the other hand, reflects the tastes and values of those making the intergenerational transfer. In a political decision setting, rather than simply calculating a net present value of benefits minus costs as occurs in integrated assessment models, the present value of the risk reduction costs to be borne by the current generation could be presented to decisionmakers and the public along with estimates of the ultimate effects (monetary and otherwise) of risk reduction and their incidence in time and space. Decisionmakers and others then have to weigh whether the benefits justify the costs.[2] This approach may offer one possibility for bridging the gap between economic net benefits calculus and ethical considerations which figures so prominently in debates over discounting and long-term environmental threats like climate change.

ENDNOTES

1. See Arrow and others 1996. A similar conclusion follows if the aggregate costs of climate change are weighted according to their incidence on rich and poor, taking into account the higher proportional loss of well-being for the poor from a negative impact (Azar and Sterner 1996).

2. For further development of this approach, see Kopp, Krupnick, and Toman 1997.

REFERENCES

Arrow, Kenneth J., William R. Cline, Karl-Göran Mäler, Mohan Munasinghe, Raymond Squitieri, and Joseph E. Stiglitz. 1996. Intertemporal Equity, Discounting, and Economic Efficiency. In James P. Bruce, Hoesung Lee, and Erik F. Haites (eds.), *Climate Change 1995—Economic and Social Dimensions of Climate Change*. Contribution of Working Group III to the Second Assessment Report of the IPCC. New York: Cambridge University Press.

Azar, Christian, and Thomas Sterner. 1996. Discounting and Distributional Considerations in the Context of Global Warming. *Ecological Economics* 19 (November): 169–94.

Howarth, Richard H. 1996. Climate Change and Overlapping Generations. *Contemporary Economic Policy* 14 (October): 100–11.

Kneese, A. V., and W. D. Schulze. 1985. Ethics and Environmental Economics. In *Handbook of Natural Resource and Energy Economics*, A. V. Kneese and J. L. Sweeney, eds. Amsterdam: North–Holland.

Kolstad, Charles A. 1996. Learning and Stock Effects in Environmental Regulation: The Case of Greenhouse Gas Emissions. *Journal of Environmental Economics and Management* 31(1, July): 1–18.

Kopp, Raymond J., Alan Krupnick, and Michael A. Toman. 1997. Cost-Benefit Analysis and Regulatory Reform. *Human and Ecological Risk Assessment* 3 (November): 787–852.

Ramsey, F. P. 1928. A Mathematical Theory of Saving. *Economic Journal* 38: 543–49. Reprinted in *Foundations: Essays in Philosophy, Logic, Mathematics, and Economics*. Edited by D. H. Mellor. 261–81.

Schelling, Thomas C. 1995. Intergenerational Discounting. *Energy Policy* 23 (April/May): 395–401.

Stiglitz, Joseph. 1974. Growth with Exhaustible Natural Resources: Efficient and Optimal Growth Paths. *Review of Economic Studies Symposium on the Economics of Exhaustible Resources* 41: 123–37. Edinburgh: Longman Group Limited.

5

On the Uses of Benefit-Cost Reasoning in Choosing Policy toward Global Climate Change

David F. Bradford

If economists could manage to get themselves thought of as humble, competent people, on a level with dentists, that would be splendid.
—John Maynard Keynes

To understand discounting, and the application of benefit-cost reasoning more generally, in the context of setting policy toward global climate change, it may be helpful to start with an easier case. In the 1980s, voluntary export restraint (VER) arrangements applied to trade in automobiles between Japan and the United States. It is estimated that the effect was to raise the prices of Japanese automobiles sold in the United States on average about $1,500 over what they would otherwise have been (Feenstra 1988). Presumably as a result of the policy, the price in the United States of automobiles manufactured in countries other than Japan, including the United States, was also somewhat higher than otherwise. Consequently, owing to the VER, U.S. buyers of automobiles suffered a loss of some significant amount, relative to the status quo. Those involved in the automobile industry, including owners of U.S.-based companies and their employees, as well as owners of Japanese companies and their employees, gained an amount roughly comparable to what U.S. consumers lost. The gains to the gainers presumably fell short of the loss to the losers, however. This is because production took place where it was more costly and because there was distortion in the composition of the output of automobiles.

DAVID F. BRADFORD is Professor of Economics and Public Affairs, Princeton University and Adjunct Professor of Law, New York University.

Was the VER a good policy? What would benefit-cost analysis have to say? The bottom line of a benefit-cost analysis would be a measure of the net gain in the aggregate, encompassing all affected parties. This total would compare the outcome under the policy with the outcome (counterfactual) under the status quo. An important question is, outcome for whom? Let us suppose the analysis is global. Everyone's benefits and costs count.

As I have suggested, the net benefit of the policy in this case was probably negative from a global perspective (and certainly so from a national perspective). In the language of policy analysis, the policy failed the benefit-cost test and resulted in a "welfare loss." A hard-line advocate of benefit-cost as a decision criterion would say that the policy, therefore, should not have been implemented. I believe there is a reasonable case to be made for adopting a benefit-cost test as a decision criterion, or at least a presumptive criterion. But the strict logic of what we learn from the benefit-cost exercise does not allow us to draw any conclusion about whether a policy that passes the test *should* be implemented. Nor does it tell us whether a policy that fails the test *should* be rejected. For somewhat similar reasons, passing a benefit-cost test is neither necessary nor sufficient to predict whether a policy will be accepted in the actual political process.

The reason is well known, but sometimes forgotten. The simple aggregate of benefits and costs does not tell us anything about who enjoys the benefits or bears the costs. In the case of the VER, beneficiaries were stakeholders in the automobile industry, especially in the United States and Japan. The losers were U.S. consumers. Economic science does not tell us whether the resulting redistribution of wealth—from U.S. consumers to stakeholders in the automobile industry—was good or bad.

The fact that the aggregate net benefit of the policy was negative does, however, contain some useful information. It tells us that there was an alternative policy to the VER that would have been better for everyone. That is, a team of economists could have dreamed up an alternative way to deliver the positive benefits to the auto industry's stakeholders at a lower cost to U.S. consumers. Whether the required alternative policy would have been in accord with the U.S. Constitution, or acceptable to a majority of the members of the House of Representatives, or explicable to David Brinkley are questions on which economics is silent. (There is a pretty strong presumption among economists—call it optimism—that if a way could have been found that satisfied such political constraints and that did give a better deal to everyone, it would have been adopted.)

Notice that to undertake this analysis, no information is needed about who ought to get more or less, who is more or less deserving. Nor is it other than a technical question what prices should be used to evaluate the changes in consumption of the various people with an interest in the outcomes—auto workers and auto buyers, for example. These are matters about which there is plenty of room to argue—does the degree of monopoly in the automobile or other markets affect the way one should value changes in the outcomes?—but the issues are not at a deep philosophical level.

To go further, to say that a policy is a good or bad thing, requires us to weigh the gains to the gainers and the losses to the losers. In the utilitarian tradition, I am inclined to apply as a rough metric the sort of "declining marginal social utility of consumption" that is the usual justification for policies that distribute from richer to poorer. I try, however, to keep straight that this is my metric, or maybe even the dominant metric in my group of professional colleagues, not one based in value-free science.

There are, however, other ways to deal with the distributional aspect of policies that would permit us to go further on a more scientific basis. First, one might argue that routinely basing decisions on the aggregate net benefits will produce, on average for everyone, a better result than case-by-case decisions in a political setting. The free enterprise economy chooses projects on essentially benefit-cost grounds. The fact that competitors will lose if I bring out a superior mousetrap does not affect my decision to do so. It would not be easy to write down a convincing model of recurring decision situations to prove rigorously that obeying the benefit-cost criterion produced a better result on average than alternative methods. But the success of competitive systems in raising living standards, by comparison with other systems, suggests that the idea is not to be dismissed out of hand either.

A stronger presumption for the benefit-cost standard obtains if distributional concerns can be summed up in terms of something like "earning power" or "ability to pay" and a tax and transfer system is in place that aims to choose the best feasible outcome in terms of this measure. If "you," the decisionmaker, are also in charge of the tax-transfer system, to a first approximation you will want to make allocative decisions, such as whether to invoke VER, on the basis of benefit-cost calculus. (Again, there are many technical caveats, but I believe the basic thrust of the proposition is correct as a matter of logic, not deeper philosophy.) An alternative interpretation is descriptive, rather than prescriptive. The political process may be thought of as maintaining some sort of equilibrium in the distribution between richer and poorer. Here, richer and poorer are measured by the criteria of the tax-transfer system (for example, income as defined by the tax code). In this setting, you will tend to be correct in predicting that policies with positive net benefits will be adopted.

Notice, however, that the condition of a redistributive tax-transfer system based on the criterion of who ought to have the greater weight in the decision did not apply in the VER case. The gainers from the policy were not identified by their income but rather by their connection to an industry (and geographical region). Since we may presume that the gains to the Japanese companies and workers did not get much weight in the calculus of U.S. decisionmakers, we must guess that the relative weights on the U.S. residents in different locations were unrelated to income as defined by the tax and welfare systems. So benefit-cost reasoning leads to a bad prediction of the outcome. The outcome chosen by taking the criterion of maximizing net benefits in the aggregate would also have been wrong from an ethical point of view, if one accepts the political equilibrium as expressing a social judgment of equity.

Let us apply the lessons of this simple example to the very different case of global climate change. The starting point is some notion of the baseline policy path. This is not a wholly obvious concept. Does the baseline path incorporate any sort of corrective adjustment in response to changing circumstances? It is usual to invoke a business-as-usual path that is a more or less well-specified version of doing what we are now doing. Alternatives are then considered, typically achieving reduced emissions of greenhouse gases by one or another set of mechanisms. An estimate is then developed of the value of period-by-period benefits, which may be due to bad things avoided, such as flooding, species destruction, and so forth. These are netted against the costs, which may be due to greater sacrifice to production of things that take energy or forgone good effects of climate change, such as higher agricultural productivity in northern regions. The thing evaluated in any given period will, incidentally, not be a fixed outcome, but rather a probability distribution of outcomes, depending on resolution of the many sources of uncertainty that inevitably attend projections into the future.

This is a formidable research problem (which is not to suggest that pulling apart the VER is child's play). To focus on the matter of discounting, let us suppose, however, it has been satisfactorily solved. We have, for each time point, the equivalent in dollars to the impact of the policy, relative to the status quo, for everybody around at the time. How should we aggregate these quantities for our benefit-cost analysis? Neglecting technical quibbles that I believe are not likely to upset the story very much, we should do the same thing we did in the VER case. There, we used the going prices for food, shelter, automobiles, and so forth to evaluate the changes in consumption of the various interested parties. Here, we would use the market prices for assets with the same profiles of returns to price out the quantities obtaining at different times.

One issue that is usually raised in connection with discounting is dealing with risk. I have attempted to integrate this issue into my description of an ideal benefit-cost analysis. The thing to be evaluated is the impact of a policy on the probability distribution of outcomes experienced by people in the future. If the impact is like a risky security, it should be evaluated as such. It is, however, important to remember that the fact that a security has a highly variable outcome does not reduce its value if its variability is inversely related to other risky outcomes. We call such a security an insurance policy.

It is an understatement to say that we can have little confidence in predictions about economic affairs many decades in the future. In making our best guesses about the impact of climate policy on the distant future, however, it is the correlation with the distribution in the absence of policy that counts. Interventions to moderate climate change will work to pay off more when the outcome would otherwise be worse. Therefore, considerations of risk are likely to affect the calculation of net benefits in a way similar to reducing the discount rate used in the analysis.

When I say that our best guess of asset market prices "should" be used in the analysis, the force of the "should" is logical, not ethical. That is, by using market prices we obtain a result that allows us to answer the question, could we combine implementation of the policy in question (for example, cutting emissions of carbon dioxide by switching to nuclear fuel) with redistribution to make everyone better off? As in the case of the VER, this is, strictly speaking, the question that economics can claim to answer. As in the case of the VER, there is no necessary implication that a policy that fails this test is "bad" and should not be adopted. Someone might claim that, the way life really works, the policy will affect the distribution of well-being. The induced changes in wealth will not be adjusted by the tax-transfer function of government, or, at least, will not be adjusted in the dimension of particular concern to this observer. The beneficiaries in the process will be particularly worthy and the losers less deserving, so a project that fails the test is a good thing on balance. This apparently described the VER for the U.S. Congress.

There seems to be a presumption in connection with global climate change that policies undertaken today will benefit future generations at the cost of consumption sacrificed by present generations. That is, distributional consequences are inextricably bound to the allocational issue of controlling greenhouse emissions. This connection is, however, not logically necessary. Suppose there were adequate means of adjusting the outcomes for their distributional effects. Then the same presumption in favor of the benefit-cost criterion in making decisions would apply to choice of policies toward global warming as in other areas.

What would such a redistributional procedure involve? Consider the content of a benefit estimate. A typical specification would be the amount of money the affected person would pay to obtain the impact in question, rather than experience the business-as-usual world. (If the mitigating policy were taken as the baseline, the benefit estimate would be the amount one would require to receive to be compensated for not obtaining the impact in question.) For example, a population that would have to move to a higher location, or build dikes, or suffer higher risks of loss of life due to severe storms would be prepared to pay some amount for an insurance policy that would mitigate these effects. The redistribution required to offset the adoption of a policy of mitigation would be a transfer away from this population toward people who would be negatively affected by the policy—presumably those living today who would sacrifice as a result of, say, a carbon tax. "Transfer away" would take the form of reducing the inheritance of the group reaping the benefit of the policy.

Apart from its apparent mean-spiritedness, this description suggests the part of the puzzle that is lacking to make benefit-cost analysis a likely sufficient guide to action or a likely predictor of political acceptance of mitigating policies. It may be reasonable to think that there is a systematic redistributive mechanism in place within the United States, both at a given time and over time. However, there is clearly no such mechanism connecting results at great geographical distance, either now or over time.

In the case of the VER, the aggregate of benefits net of costs proved a bad predictor of the collective choice. Taking the congressional judgment as the measure of social welfare, it also proved a bad indicator of the socially better choice. For much the same reason, the aggregate net benefit of climate change, whether correctly discounted or not, is unlikely to provide enough information for either predicting or guiding choices. What must be added is information about the distribution of gains and losses, over time and across space.

By doing so, we would draw attention to the potential for developing compensating changes that might be necessary to make a policy that would otherwise be vetoed by a losing group acceptable politically. We could, for example, run larger budget deficits to reduce the inheritance of future generations. We might be induced to sympathize with a population distant in time and place if we were convinced they would be very poor and that they could be helped by our sacrifice today.

My remarks about discounting presuppose that it has been sensible or feasible to translate the impacts of policies into monetary terms. It seems to me that this is the toughest part. The hard question is how to value the possible annihilation of species or the flooding of areas of human settlement. It is not likely that we can be completely successful assigning money values to such impacts. To be sure, at some level, we make such implicit trade-offs every day. Decisions about public safety, national defense, intervention in foreign wars or natural disasters, and any number of other matters of high and low policy require balancing of money costs and nonmonetary benefits. Benefit-cost analysis can, at best, help us put such matters in perspective. An example would be comparing the costs of saving a statistical life by mandating seat-belt use and regulating the cleanup of abandoned waste dumps.

One has to be impressed with the uncertainty that exists about the shape of human civilization in two or three hundred years. What would we have said in 1775 if we happened to live in the British colonies on the East Coast of North America about what life would look like in the same place in 1996? What can we now say about what life will look like here, or in the Middle East, or sub-Saharan Africa in 2150? With this vagueness about the distant future in mind, let me conclude with a brief response to the four questions posed to us by the conveners:

- We have no real choice but to treat projects whose effects will be spread out over hundreds of years as longer versions of projects having impacts over a mere forty years.
- To a first approximation, the appropriate way to discount probability distributions of consumption for purposes of determining a policy's potential for making everybody better off is to use market discount rates appropriate for the distributions in questions.
- Because no mechanisms exist for adjusting the distribution of gains and losses more or less automatically, to assess a policy requires information about gains and losses of specific groups or cohorts through time. The most practical way to describe such distributive effects is in terms of the value of consumption, discounted to the present. These are the magnitudes we need to know to assess the alternative distributions of benefits and costs that are available. The effects cannot be reliably added together, however.
- If its logic is well understood, benefit-cost analysis should be very helpful in decisionmaking on even such complex issues as global climate change. The most serious problem is evaluating hard-to-value things. Many policy alternatives, such as the choice of instrument to control greenhouse gas emissions, do not raise such difficult questions.

ACKNOWLEDGMENTS

In the spirit of the exercise as it was presented to the authors of the original papers for the workshop, I have omitted references to the literature. I would, however, like to acknowledge a particular debt to Thomas Schelling's essay, "Intergenerational Discounting" (Schelling 1995).

REFERENCES

Feenstra, Robert C. 1988. Quality Change Under Trade Restraints in Japanese Autos. *Quarterly Journal of Economics* CIII-1(February): 131–46.

Schelling, Thomas C. 1995. Intergenerational Discounting. *Energy Policy* 23(4–5): 395–401.

6

A Market-Based Discount Rate

Comments on Bradford

W. David Montgomery

David Bradford's paper is one of the rare contributions to the literature on intergenerational discounting that both is consistent with theoretical welfare economics and makes practical sense as a guide to policy. He also manages to do this without ever appealing to a social welfare function to provide an ultimate moral standard.

Bradford makes four points:

- We frequently observe policies that do not pass a benefit-cost test being adopted because they benefit particular groups. Maximizing net benefits is neither a necessary nor a sufficient condition for policy choice.
- Benefit-cost analysis identifies potential Pareto improvements—outcomes in which it is possible to make everyone better off—but it only estimates net gains or losses in the aggregate. It also matters how costs and benefits are distributed.
- If the decisionmaker on the policy in question also controls a tax and transfer system for redistributing income, then the decisionmaker will want to maximize net benefits when choosing policies because distributional issues can be handled separately.
- The application of benefit-cost analysis can show what is being sacrificed to provide benefits to specific groups through inefficient policy design.

W. David Montgomery is Vice President of Charles River Associates in Washington, D.C.

How do these very sensible and correct remarks apply to the choice of discount rate? Bradford makes this connection by pointing out that market prices for assets (in particular, market interest rates) must be used in evaluating climate-change policies if we want to answer the question, could we combine implementation of the policy in question (for example, cutting emissions of carbon dioxide by switching to nuclear fuel) with redistribution to make everyone better off? Using discount rates in this context has nothing to do with ethics, as long as there are alternative ways of making provisions for future generations.

In earlier writings on discount rates for energy policy, Joseph Stiglitz made exactly the same point. Except for very special cases in which the government's ability to tax and to affect the distribution of income across generations is constrained, he found that it is necessary to use market-determined interest rates as the "social rate of discount" to achieve an efficient outcome. Using any other discount rate violates the intertemporal efficiency conditions and implies that there is a different policy that will make all generations better off than the policy that is optimal under the lower discount rate. Basically, using something other than the market discount rate means sacrificing efficiency to achieve some desired distributive goals.

This point is so fundamental that it is worth elaborating. In Figure 1, I have drawn a standard utility possibility frontier representing the maximum utility it is possible to provide to the future for any specified level of present utility. Each point on this frontier satisfies the intertemporal efficiency conditions, which (to state them simply in the current context) require that all projects pass a benefit-cost test based on market interest rates. I have also drawn, with regret, a social welfare function that expresses moral judgments about how utility should be allocated between current and future generations. I will return to the interesting question of whose social welfare function this is.

With no emission limits, utility for both generations will be within the frontier—indicating that there are some emission limits whose net benefits at market rates would exceed their costs. Using market rates to evaluate policies to reduce emissions might move utility to the point labeled "market discount rate outcome"—a point on the utility possibility frontier at which the current generation does have reduced utility and the future generation gains.

This point may not give enough welfare to the future, based on some moral judgment expressed in some social welfare function. If totally nondistorting means were used to transfer utility from current to future generations, the result would be a "first best outcome" according to this utility function.

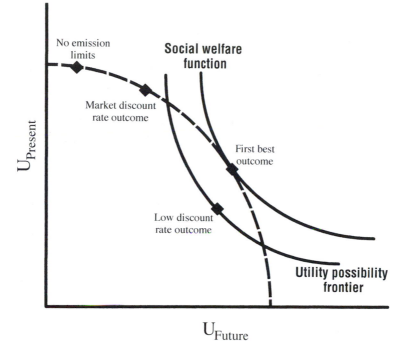

Figure 1. Current and Future Welfare.

It is worth noting that there are, indeed, ways to make transfers to future generations that not only are nondistorting but would actually benefit current generations. For example, virtually all public finance and tax economists have concluded that changes in tax law and fiscal policy to reduce budget deficits and encourage saving and capital formation would provide such benefits, because current tax and fiscal policies are so far skewed to discourage saving and investment. Thus, there is readily at hand a set of tax and fiscal reforms that would bring about exactly the improvement in welfare for future generations that proponents of social discount rates below market rates desire.

If tax and transfer policies are constrained, it may be impossible to reach the utility possibility frontier. In this case, an adherent to the moral sentiments in the social welfare function drawn earlier might wish to sacrifice some efficiency to reach a preferred distribution. This is labeled the "low discount rate outcome." It is inside the utility possibility frontier, reflecting the fact that use of market rates is a necessary condition for intertemporal efficiency. This outcome could only be desired if there is no better way to transfer income to future generations (and if the moral sentiments in the social welfare function are determinative of public policy).

I would actually go further than Bradford in urging the importance of using market interest rates to calculate the policies to reduce emissions. A great deal of work is now being done on the question of what time profile of emission reductions will achieve stated concentration goals at least cost. For this analysis of optimal timing, it is critically important that market interest rates, reflecting the opportunity costs of expenditures to reduce emissions, are used. It is only in evaluating the benefits of reducing emissions that the issue of intergenerational discounting and social discount rates should arise. The question of distribution between generations comes up only in choosing the concentration goal, not in determining how to achieve that goal at least cost. Since most sensitivity analyses show that the most important information for current decisions is on the timing issue rather than on the ultimate goal, use of market rates is critical to avoid mistaken conclusions about the optimal time path for emission reduction.

I would also hesitate to go as far as Bradford in adjusting discount rates to account for risk. When time scales for costs and benefits differ so drastically, the classic Arrow and Lind argument for adjusting the price to deal with risk applies. I think this is consistent with Bradford's other recommendations about getting the price to be applied to environmental damages right and leaving the discount rate alone.

One of Bradford's most important recommendations is that we evaluate the trade-offs between intertemporal efficiency and distributive goals by displaying time paths of consumption or welfare with and without climate policy. I think these can be very informative, in terms of how much better off future generations will be relative to current generations, and how much difference it makes to their welfare whether or not we engage in emission reductions currently. If a decisionmaker really does carry a social welfare function around in his or her head, that social welfare function can be applied to the time paths of consumption or welfare to decide on how much to reduce emissions. Casual inspection of the time paths may also reveal a great deal about the issue, since I believe they will show present welfare reductions that significantly exceed future welfare gains, and future welfare under current policy far larger than current welfare.

Finally, there is the question of whose social welfare function should be used in deciding whether to incur efficiency losses to achieve some intergenerational distribution unattainable by means other than climate policy.

I would argue that the social rate of time preference revealed in current tax and fiscal policies throughout the industrialized world is high. Rates of investment and economic growth are much lower than a Ramsey model based on low discount rates would predict (as pointed out by Alan Manne) and current tax and fiscal policies actively discourage saving and capital formation. No decisionmaker with the social welfare function posited by Stiglitz would tolerate the U.S. tax code, or even pay attention to climate issues until that tax code was fixed. Since we see no great rush to move the tax code in this direction, I conclude that the U.S. government does not share the social welfare function posited. This means that recommendations based on some arbitrary social welfare function for policies that an immortal decisionmaker would care about only with a negligible discount rate truly are counsels of perfection. That may be a task for moralists, philosophers, or others who see their job as changing the morals and ethics of their generation. For more modest economists who simply want to help policymakers and individuals achieve the best outcome given their current objectives and preferences, the right discount rate is the one recommended by Bradford—one based on market rates.

7

Intergenerational Equity, Social Discount Rates, and Global Warming

Partha Dasgupta, Karl-Göran Mäler, and Scott Barrett

This paper is about the logic underlying social discount rates. We argue that these rates are not ethical raw material but are derived from the more fundamental notion of justice among generations. A number of approaches to the concept of intergenerational justice are discussed, and it is argued that the most compelling formulation available to us is the one that has long been in use among economists, namely, the Ramsey-Koopmans theory. This theory advocates that investment projects having long-run effects should be subjected to the same conceptual treatment as those that affect only the near future. We show that social discount rates depend on the numeraire, and that methods of estimating them depend on the institutional setting within which social benefit-cost analysis is assumed to be undertaken. We also show that it is incorrect to advocate project-specific discount rates as a way of conserving environmental resources.

Social discount rates have universally been taken to be positive, on the grounds that the rate of return on investment is positive. But, if consumption and production activities give rise to environmental pollution

PARTHA DASGUPTA is the Frank Ramsey Professor of Economics at the University of Cambridge. KARL-GÖRAN MÄLER is a professor of economics at the Stockholm School of Economics. All are associated with the Beijer International Institute of Ecological Economics of the Royal Academy of Sciences, Stockholm. SCOTT BARRETT is Associate Professor of Economics at the London School of Business.

as a by-product, the social rate of return on investment could be zero even when the private rate is positive; at the very least, the social rate would be lower than the private rate. The current practice among most global energy modelers of relying exclusively on (risk-free) market rates of return for estimating optimal carbon taxes is conceptually faulty. In the context of a formal model of environmental pollution, we show how, even along an optimal program, social rates of discount can be zero. We also demonstrate that in certain institutional settings, social discount rates can be negative.

WHAT ARE SOCIAL DISCOUNT RATES AND HOW MIGHT WE ESTIMATE THEM?

Imagine a public authority engaged in an intertemporal optimization exercise—say, on the choice of the aggregate rate of investment in an economy. We will assume that the authority is morally at ease with the social welfare function it is charged with maximizing and is confident that it has taken both technological and institutional constraints effectively into account. The institutional constraints consist of, among other things, the responses of private bodies and other public authorities to its decisions. So, depending on the context, the extent to which the authority in question can influence the economy may be great or small.

It is a well-known fact that, under certain circumstances, the optimal program can be decentralized.[1] By this we mean that there is a set of *accounting prices* that, if used in the evaluation of small investment projects, could sustain the optimal program (Arrow and Kurz 1970; Little and Mirrlees 1974).[2] Thus, investment projects are perturbations to the macroeconomy (see the penultimate section of this paper detailing a model of global warming); the criterion for project selection is social profitability; and the social profitabilities of projects are estimated on the basis of accounting prices, not market prices.

Accounting prices are state-contingent. And, it is on this point that the theory on which we are relying is weak: the theory of choice under uncertainty, particularly the kind of uncertainty that makes possibilities in the distant future only dimly visible, is relatively undeveloped. Certain precautionary considerations, such as the value of keeping options open, do follow from the classical expected-utility theory (Arrow and Fisher 1974; Henry 1974); these features are, of course, a plus for the theory. On the other hand, the expected-utility theory runs into difficulties when used in the evaluation of projects with long-term effects. For example, it may simply not be possible today to evaluate environmental risks in the distant future. Bewley (1989) has developed an interpretation of Knightian uncertainty that offers a reason why we ought to be reluctant to undertake activities involving unevaluatable risks; that is, why the status quo should be favored. But, these are early days for such theories as Bewley's. At the moment, we do not have a theory, normative or otherwise, that would cover long-term environmental uncertainties in a satisfactory way. So, in what follows, we will ignore uncertainty. If this appears otiose, readers can imagine that we are working within the expected-utility framework.

Let a numeraire be chosen for the accounting price system. At any given date, the *social rate of discount* is the percentage rate at which the accounting price of the numeraire declines. Formally, let R_t be the quantity of the numeraire you must pay today for a unit of the numeraire to be delivered at time t along the optimal program. Assuming continuous time and a differentiable accounting price, $-[dR_t/dt]/R_t$ is the social rate of discount at t.

The basis of the definition is this: a repeated use of social discount rates across time enables us to compute social discount factors, which can, in turn, be used to convert the spot prices of various goods and services in the future into their present-value prices. This means, of course, that, when we speak of a project's social profitability, as we have already done, we mean the present discounted value of the project's flow of net social profits.

One immediate corollary is that social discount rates, typically, depend on the numeraire (see the third section of this paper on intergenerational social welfare functions). The reason is that, unless the optimal program is a steady state, relative spot prices change over time. However, project selection is unaffected by the choice of numeraire. Projects that are socially profitable (or, respectively, unprofitable) with one numeraire would remain socially profitable (or, respectively, unprofitable) if the numeraire were something else.

A second immediate corollary is that, typically, social discount rates are not constant over time; they vary over time. In other words, except under special circumstances, the accounting price of a numeraire does not decline at a constant exponential rate (again, see the third section of this paper). The near-universal practice of using a constant discount rate in project evaluation (for example, 5% per year applied to the net income of a project over its entire life) has grown out of a need for practical convenience; it is not a theoretical prescription.

A third immediate corollary is that social discount rates are not project specific: the same set of discount rates should be used in the evaluation of all projects. For example, if society were to value biodiversity greatly, it would, rightly, expect this concern to be reflected in the social profitability of such projects as those that protect biodiversity. It is, on occasion, suggested that preferential discount rates ought to be used in the evaluation of such projects, to make them look good. But the suggestion is wrong. If society were to value biodiversity greatly, this concern would be reflected in the accounting prices of biodiversity in the future; they would be high, and the magnitude of biodiversity loss in the future, even when discounted to the present, would be large.

A fourth immediate corollary is that, because social discount rates connect accounting prices at different dates, they are a derived notion. Reflecting as they do both the possible and the desirable, social rates of discount are not ethical raw material; they are endogenously determined within the optimization exercise.[3]

Thus far, an optimizing institution. An extreme special case of it is one in which the choice of investment projects is conceived of as a sequence of *reforms*. The thought experiment here is that small investment projects are chosen one at a time, in a sequential manner. Accounting prices in this scheme of things are estimated from the prevailing structure of production and consumption, at each stage of the sequence; they are not obtained from an optimal program. However, social rates of discount in this context connect accounting prices at different dates in the same manner as in the optimizing institution: at any date the social discount rate is defined as the percentage rate at which the accounting price of the numeraire declines.

Consider now a sequence of choices: at each stage, small investment projects are evaluated at the marginal social valuations of goods and services at that stage, and only socially profitable projects are accepted. Such a process of choice is called a "gradient process." Under certain conditions (namely, when the economy satisfies strong convexity properties), a sequence of project selections obeying a gradient process eventually leads the economy to the optimal program.[4]

There is a third institutional framework within which project choice can be studied. Here, the focus is on some small sector of an economy. Assume that project selection in the sector is conducted optimally. Being a small sector, decisions made within it leave the rest of the economy unaffected. This is the world of partial equilibrium. Social rates of discount in such exercises are exogenously given: they are not determined from the optimization exercise, they are inferred from a forecast of the behavior of the rest of the economy. Early models of global warming were cast in such a mold (for example, Nordhaus 1977). These models were instructive. But, "partial equilibrium" models are an inappropriate arena in which to build models of global warming, because global warming is expected to have economywide effects on production possibilities; indeed, worldwide effects. This means that the welfare economics of global warming needs to be developed in the context of optimizing economies. This is done by Nordhaus (1994) and Nordhaus and Yang (1996).[5]

We began by observing that if public authorities are to optimize, they must be able to evaluate alternatives by means of a social welfare function. A prior question is whether a public authority is at all needed for reaching good investment decisions. To ask the question another way, does mere temporal distance between us and future people provide a reason why we cannot trust our private preferences to be ethical? In short, does temporal distance imply empathetic distance?

US VERSUS THE FUTURE: PARENTAL CONCERN AS A RECURSIVE RELATION

A vast literature on optimal economic development (for example, Chakravarty 1969) would suggest that it does provide a reason. The literature gives the impression that future generations are at risk from the present's lack of a natural concern for them; so that if deliberative collective action were not taken, say, through the agency of a public authority, the present would blow its inherited wealth. The thought here is that future generations cannot bargain with us, nor can they remind us of our obligations to them. Their absence today is a reason why they are at risk from our rapacity.

We are talking here of a possible lack of both moral and instinctive motivation to care for future generations, we are not referring to the constraints that may prevent us individually from investing the amounts we would ideally like to invest (for example, because capital markets are imperfect or because many of our actions give rise to current and future externalities or whatever; see the penultimate section of this paper that details the model of global warming). And, when we recognize this distinction (that is, the distinction between what we desire on reflection and what we are able to achieve), we begin to doubt whether we are as rapacious as the literature on economic development often suggests we are. There are people who feel that their ancestors saved too much for the future; that they should have sacrificed less for their descendants. To be sure, it is not unacknowledged by such people that, in the process, their ancestors also damaged many ecosystems. But, this could have been due to ineffectual property rights over such resources; it need not have reflected a lack of concern on the part of the ancestors for their descendants. For example, the standard of living in Western Europe has increased more than eightfold since the start of the Industrial Revolution. This happened through an accumulation of physical, human, intellectual, and organizational capital (and, almost certainly, a concomitant decumu-

lation of natural capital). To look at the contemporary world, gross investment rates in East Asian countries have been well in excess of 30% for
some time now. It is doubtful whether this has all been due to the visible
hand of government, or from life-cycle, precautionary motives. But, if this
doubt is warranted, where does the intergenerational concern come
from?

Some economists (for example, Barro and Becker 1989; Dasgupta
1974) have explored the thought that, leaving aside their external effects
(for example, contributing to global warming by one's consumption and
production activities), savings decisions do not involve social ethics. They
have suggested that considerate parents take into account the well-being
of their children when deciding how much to save. If they are, in addition, thoughtful parents, they know that the welfare of their children will
depend on the well-being of their children, that the welfare of their children will, in turn, depend on the well-being of their children, and so on,
down the generations. In short, or so it has been argued, there is a natural
recursion of well-being interests along a family line.[6] Thus, thoughtful
parents can be expected to take account of the interests of their distant
descendants indirectly, even when they are directly interested only in
their own children.

To see how the argument works, consider generation t (≥ 0) of a family line, or dynasty. The present is denoted by $t = 0$ and time is discrete.
For simplicity of exposition, assume that population is constant; and to
make certain there are no hidden externalities, let us normalize the population size to one in each period. A person lives for precisely one period.
Assume now that each person's well-being depends on her own consumption level and on her offspring's well-being. Denote the well-being
of generation t by W_t. Writing by C_t her consumption of goods and services, we may express W_t as a function of C_t and W_{t+1}:

$$W_t = W(C_t, W_{t+1}) \tag{1}$$

This is a recursive relation. The problem is that, as it stands, it is far
too general to offer us any insights. So, we seek to simplify. The simplest
thing by far is to assume that W_t is of the form

$$W_t = U(C_t) + \phi W_{t+1}, \text{ with } 1 \geq \phi > 0 \tag{2}$$

where $U(C_t)$ is an increasing function of C_t and ϕ (a constant) is a time discount factor.[7]

Repeated use of expression (2) then implies that

$$W_0 = \Sigma_0^\infty \phi^t U(C_t) \tag{3a}$$

and, more generally, that for generation t (≥ 0),

$$W_t = \Sigma_t{}^\infty \phi^{(\tau-t)} U(C_\tau) \tag{3b}$$

Even though equation (3b) looks like the classical utilitarian formula for generation t, it is not so: the function $U(.)$ does not necessarily possess the interpretation that classical utilitarians placed on the notion of utility.

Parental concerns in (3a) extend into the indefinite future. However, it has, on occasion, been suggested—if only implicitly (Rawls 1972)—that this reflects more concern than is typically displayed by parents for the welfare of their descendants. With this in mind, alternative motivation assumptions have been explored in the economics literature (Dasgupta 1974). A simple form of a truncated W_t is

$$W_t = U(C_t) + \phi U(C_{t+1}), \text{ for } t \geq 0 \tag{4}$$

A natural generalization of equation (4) involves parents caring only about their own consumption and the consumption rates of the T generations that are to follow them (Arrow 1973): [8]

$$W_t = \Sigma_t{}^{t+T} \phi^{(\tau-t)} U(C_\tau) \tag{5}$$

Schelling (1995, 396) has suggested a different formulation. He has speculated that "...time may serve as a kind of measure of 'distance.' ... Beyond certain distances there may be no further depreciation for time, culture, geography, race, or kinship."

Phelps and Pollak (1968) had explored a similar idea. They assumed

$$W_t = U(C_t) + \kappa \Sigma_{t+1}{}^\infty \phi^{(\tau-t)} U(C_\tau) \tag{6}$$

where $1 \geq \phi > 0$ and $1 > \kappa > 0$. Expression (6) reduces to Schelling's suggested form if $\phi = 1$.

Observe that, in expression (6), the marginal rate of substitution between U at $t+1$ and U at $t+2$, when evaluated at t, differs from the rate of substitution when evaluated at $t+1$. This is another way of saying that expression (6) embodies incoherent concerns among generations. So, the inevitable next question is, how would the incoherence be expected to be accommodated?

It is difficult to imagine that generations can reach a binding agreement over such an object as aggregate saving. So, one is led to study noncooperative equilibriums of intergenerational savings games. In the context of a simple, one-commodity production model (Ramsey 1928), Phelps and Pollak (1968) did just that. They showed that if intergenerational concern is reflected by expression (6), stationary noncooperative equilibrium savings rules are Pareto-inefficient. Dasgupta (1974) used the simpler form, equation (4), to show that *all* noncooperative equilibrium savings rules are Pareto-inefficient.

We would appear to have reached an impasse. We must go elsewhere if we are to arrive at a language for justice among generations.

We began this account with parental concerns. But if parents are thoughtful, they will ask what concern they *ought* to display toward their descendants. This leads to welfare economics. So, we turn to it.

INTERGENERATIONAL SOCIAL WELFARE FUNCTIONS AND THEIR SOCIAL DISCOUNT RATES[9]

Rawls (1972) offered us reasons for taking seriously extreme equity in the distribution of what he called "primary goods." The concept of primary goods has spawned a large philosophical literature since his book was published. However, in their attempts to apply Rawls' insights to the problem of optimal saving, economists cut through philosophical knots by interpreting W_t in equations (3)–(5) as a primary good. As is well known, Rawls's theory of justice, when used among contemporaries, yields the (lexicographic) maxi-min principle of distribution of primary goods. What is less well appreciated is that Rawls shied away from the principle in his discussion of justice among generations. Nevertheless, it is instructive to study intergenerational maxi-min savings policies, if only to check whether Rawls was correct in discarding the maxi-min principle.

Arrow (1973) and Solow (1974b) explored savings behavior when each generation invokes the intergenerational maxi-min principle. They and Dasgupta (1974) proved that if parental concerns extend only to a finite number of descendants, as in expression (5), the principle implies either a stagnant economy (this is so if ϕ is small) or a program of savings and dissavings that would be revoked by the generation following any that were to pursue it (this is so if ϕ is not small). In the latter case, the maxi-min program is dynamically inconsistent. The Rawlsian route would appear to be unpromising.

But, justice among generations had been the object of inquiry among economists long before Rawls wrote on it. The framework in use was, and continues to be, that adopted by Ramsey (1928) and developed by Koopmans (1960, 1972). Ramsey took a straightforward utilitarian approach to the problem, while Koopmans greatly enlarged the scope of utilitarianism by adopting an axiomatic approach to the matter of intergenerational justice. We turn to Koopmans' formulation.

Time is taken to be continuous. Let population at date t (≥ 0) be denoted by L_t. We take it as exogenously given.[10] For expositional ease, we will imagine that if C_t is aggregate consumption at t, the well-being of the representative person at t is a continuous, increasing function of per capita consumption, C_t/L_t. We denote this by $U(C_t/L_t)$. We next assume that aggregate well-being at t is a function solely of $U(C_t/L_t)$ and L_t. We write this as $W_t = W(U(C_t/L_t), L_t)$.[11] The planning horizon is from the present to infinity.

Let the set of feasible consumption programs be denoted by Γ_C. We will suppose that Γ_C is uniformly bounded. Admittedly, this smacks squarely against current models of economic growth (Barro and Sala-i-Martin 1995; Romer 1996), which devise macroeconomic policies that would sustain unbounded consumption programs. But, the idea of unbounded consumption is science fiction. It ignores the environmental resource base on whose services all production and consumption ultimately depends. This base is very much finite in extent. For example, Vitousek and others (1986) have estimated that 40% of the net energy created by terrestrial photosynthesis (that is, net primary production of the biosphere) is currently being appropriated for human use. This is, of course, a very rough estimate. Moreover, net terrestrial primary production is not given exogenously, nor is it fixed; it depends, in part, on human activity. Nevertheless, the figure does put the scale of the human presence on the planet in perspective.[12]

Corresponding to each feasible C_t is a W_t. So let Γ_W be the set of feasible W_ts. For the moment, we will take it that Γ_W is also uniformly bounded.[13] Imagine next that the public authority has been provided with an ordering over Γ_W. Koopmans (1960) showed that if the ordering satisfies a set of plausible assumptions, it can be represented by the "utilitarian" form[14]

$$_0\!\int^\infty L_t \left(U(C_t/L_t)\, e^{-\delta t} \right) dt, \text{ where } \delta > 0 \tag{7}$$

Expression (7) may look like classical utilitarianism, but it is not. There is nothing in the Koopmans axioms that forces a classical utilitarian interpretation on U. It is a numerical representation of an ordering, nothing more. Economists continue to refer to U as utility, but that is more from habit than anything else.

Expression (7) involves discounting aggregate utility at a constant rate ($\delta > 0$) and integrating over their present values. If aggregate utility at $t = 0$ were the numeraire, δ would be the social rate of discount. It is often called the rate of pure time preference. Koopmans' work is illuminating because it shows whether our discounting future utilities is something that ought to be derived from more fundamental ethical principles.

It represents a radical break with a philosophical tradition, stretching from Ramsey (1928) to Parfit (1984), that has warned us against discounting future utilities without providing serious arguments.

When conducting experiments with alternative assumptions embodied in expression (7), it makes sense to go beyond the Koopmans' axioms and consider also the case, $\delta = 0$. This way, we are able to test models to see what they imply about social benefit-cost analysis. On the other hand, purposeless generality should be avoided. So we will assume that $U(C/L)$ is strictly concave, to give shape to the idea that intergenerational equity is valued as an ethical goal (see below).

It will make for expositional simplicity now if we were to suppose that population is of constant size. Thus, we will do so. In which case, we may as well normalize and set $L_t = 1$. Thus, aggregate well-being at t is $U(C_t)$. Now, recall the definition of social discount rates. If, instead of U, consumption were chosen as the numeraire, the social rate of discount would be

$$\rho_t = \rho(C_t) = \delta + \alpha(C_t)[dC_t/dt]/C_t \tag{8}$$

where $\alpha(C_t) > 0$ is the elasticity of marginal utility.[15] $\rho(C_t)$ is sometimes called the *consumption rate of interest* (Little and Mirrlees 1974). In applied benefit-cost analysis, aggregate consumption is often taken to be numeraire (for example, Dasgupta, Marglin, and Sen 1972).

In a discrete time formulation, $\rho(C_t)$ would be the marginal rate of substitution between consumption at dates t and $t+1$, minus one. Along an optimal program, this must equal the marginal rate of transformation between consumption at dates t and $t+1$, minus one. The latter is sometimes called the *social rate of return on investment*. Write it as r_t. Then, along an optimal program in continuous time, we would have

$$r_t = \delta + \alpha(C_t)[dC_t/dt]/C_t \tag{9}$$

This is the famous Ramsey Rule.

All this is familiar (see, for example, Arrow and Kurz 1970; Dasgupta and Heal 1979; Lind 1982). But, it is as well to remind ourselves that if consumption were expected to grow for a period, the consumption rate of interest would be positive even if δ were zero, an illustration of the fact that social discount rates depend on the numeraire.

Isoelastic utility functions offer a simple, flexible form of U. Consider the form[16]

$$U(C) = -C^{-(\alpha-1)}, \text{ where } \alpha > 1 \tag{10}$$

In this case, the social welfare function in equation (7) depends on only two parameters: α and δ. They reflect different concerns. α is an index of the extent to which intergenerational equity in the distribution of consumption is valued (see below). δ is, as we have seen, more directly interpretable: the larger is δ; the lower is the weight awarded to future generations' utilities relative to that of the present generation.

Let $\delta = 0$. As an example, assume that $\alpha = 2.5$ (a not implausible figure if $U(C)$ were to be based on revealed preference). If, over a period, the rate of growth of consumption at t along the optimal program is, say, 0.02% per year, then $\rho_t = 0.05$ per year during that period. That the social rate of discount depends on the numeraire is even now not appreciated in a good deal of the environmental literature that is critical of social benefit-cost analysis (for example, Daly and Cobb 1991). Modern philosophers writing on the matter also often do not appreciate it. They argue that δ should be zero and then criticize the practice of discounting future flows of consumption in social benefit-cost analysis (Cowen and Parfit 1992; Parfit 1984).

It will be noticed that the larger is α, the more egalitarian is the optimal consumption path. As $\alpha \to \infty$, the social welfare function in equation (7) looks more and more like the intergenerational maxi-min principle. This, in turn, means that, even in productive economies, optimal growth in consumption is slow if α is large [equation (9)]. In the limit, as $\alpha \to \infty$, optimal growth is zero, a supremely egalitarian outcome. From expression (9), we can see why the consumption rate of interest is bounded (and how it manages to equal the social rate of return on investment) even in these extreme parametric terrains. (On this, see Dasgupta and Heal 1979, Chapters 9 and 10.)

In equation (10), $U(C)$ is unbounded below. If $\delta = 0$, this ensures that very low consumption rates are penalized by equation (7). On the other hand, if δ were positive, low consumption rates by generations sufficiently far in the future would not be penalized by equation (7). This means that, unless the economy is sufficiently productive, optimal consumption will tend to zero in the very long run. As an illustration of how critical δ can be, Dasgupta and Heal (1974) and Solow (1974b) showed in a stylized economy with exhaustible resources that optimal consumption declines to zero in the long run if $\delta > 0$, but increases to infinity if $\delta = 0$. This was the substance of Solow's remark (Solow 1974a) that, in the economics of exhaustible resources, the choice of δ can be a matter of considerable moment.

One way of preserving something like a balance among the generations would be to maximize expression (7), subject to the constraint that the well-being of no generation falls below some acceptable level. The weakness of this approach is that side constraints do not admit trade-offs between competing goals: the accounting price of a side constraint is nil when the constraint is nonbinding, but it is positive whenever it binds. For this reason, welfare economists typically avoid side constraints as a device for avoiding morally indefensible outcomes.

An alternative would be to weaken the Koopmans axioms in some directions even while strengthening them in others, to build in directly the idea that the dictates of intergenerational fairness prohibit zero or "near-zero" consumption level for any generation. One way to do this would be to regard aggregate well-being as a weighted sum of expression (7) and the long-run average well-being over time.[17] The latter term could even be approximated by minimum requirements for long-run stocks of environmental resources, such as air and water quality, biodiversity, soil quality, and so forth. Such a hybrid formulation attempts to account for both basic human needs and resource constraints.

But, there are further problems: there always are. Schelling (1995) has reminded us that discounting one's *own* future well-being is a different matter from discounting (or "depreciating") future people's well-being. He has argued that conflating the two, as is customary in modern economics, is muddled practice.

How should we accommodate Schelling's strictures? Consider the following model (Dasgupta 1996).

Population size is constant, generations are nonoverlapping, but otherwise identical, and each generation lives for precisely t years. We may then normalize and assume that at any moment there is a single individual alive. Let each person discount his or her own utility at the rate, δ ($>$ 0). Lifetime well-being of a person just born would then be

$$\int_0^T U(C_t)e^{-\delta t}\, dt$$

and the remaining lifetime well-being of a person who has τ years still to live ($\tau < T$) would be

$$\int_0^\tau U(C_t)e^{-\delta t}\, dt$$

Assume now that no generation discounts the lifetime well-being of the generations that are to follow. This means that the social welfare function adopted at $t = 0$ by the generation born at $t = 0$ is

$$\int_0^T U(C_t)e^{-\delta t}\, dt + e^{\delta T}\int_T^{2T} U(C_t)e^{-\delta t}\, dt + e^{2\delta T}\int_{2T}^{3T} U(C_t)e^{-\delta t}\, dt + \dots \quad (11)$$

and the one adopted at T by the generation born at T is

$$\int_0^T U(C_t)e^{-\delta t}\, dt + e^{\delta T}\int_T^{2T} U(C_t)e^{-\delta t}\, dt + e^{2\delta T}\int_{2T}^{3T} U(C_t)e^{-\delta t}\, dt + \dots$$

and so forth.

What does an optimal program under equation (11) look like? Let $n = 1, 2, ...$ It is immediate that at $t \neq nT$, optimum consumption satisfies the Ramsey Rule, expression (9). But, the social welfare function in equation (11) is discontinuous at $t = nT$. It is, in fact, easy to show that consumption along the optimal program increases discontinuously at nT. (See Figure 1.)

By how much? If U is of the form (10), it can be proved that planned consumption at these discrete moments leaps by the factor, $\exp(\delta T/\alpha)$. A typical optimal consumption program is shown in the accompanying fig-ure under the assumption that the social rate of return in investment (r) exceeds δ.

Does the program look reasonable? In one sense it does. Since equa-tion (11) is something like a hybrid of two forms of the "utilitarian" social welfare function (the two forms being equation (7) with $\delta = 0$ and equa-tion (7) with $\delta > 0$), the optimal consumption program also displays

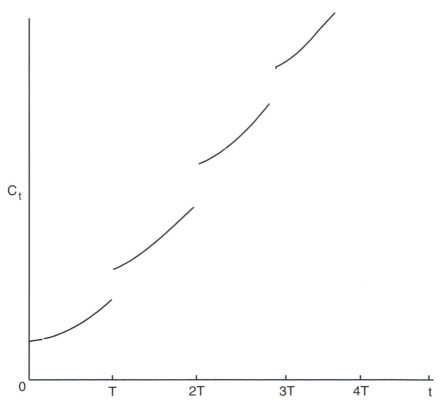

Figure 1. Discontinuous Consumption Increases in an Optimal Program.

hybrid features. On the other hand, the program is intertemporally inconsistent, so it is not self-enforcing.

To see why, consider someone who has τ years to live, where $0 < \tau < T$. The social welfare function that this someone would subscribe to reads as

$$\int_0^\tau U(C_t)e^{-\delta t}\,dt + e^{\delta\tau}\int_\tau^{\tau+T} U(C_t)e^{-\delta t}\,dt + e^{\delta(\tau+T)}\int_{\tau+T}^{\tau+2T} U(C_t)e^{-\delta t}\,dt + \dots \quad (12)$$

But equation (12) is not the social welfare function this someone sub-scribed to at an earlier stage of his or her life; nor will that someone sub-scribe to it at a later stage of his or her life. To see this sharply, notice that, as $\tau \to 0$, the person would be less and less willing to subscribe to the jump in consumption by the next generation. Thus, someone who thinks of pursuing the consumption program in the accompanying figure should know that he or she will wish constantly to step off it as time unfolds.

Intertemporal inconsistency is a serious weakness of formulation (11). So, we abandon it. In contrast, the Ramsey-Koopmans formulation in equation (7), with $\delta \geq 0$, is not unreasonable: it seems to capture the kinds of consideration that are appealing on reflection. In what follows, we will study its implications for the economics of global pollution.

THE ATMOSPHERE AS A GLOBAL COMMONS: CAN SOCIAL DISCOUNT RATES EVER BE ZERO OR NEGATIVE?

Production and consumption activities involve the emission of green-house gases as a by-product; and the atmosphere is a sink for greenhouse gases. So, the atmosphere is a global commons. There is enormous uncer-tainty about the nature and spatial distribution of the economic impacts of global warming, but there is little divergence of opinion among experts that, in the long run, there will be significant economic impacts if green-house emissions continue to increase at current rates (Houghton 1996).[18] It might then be thought that, taken together, these features imply market failure with a vengeance, and that large (Pigovian) taxes on carbon emis-sions would be required to remove the distortion. But, simulations under-taken on a model of an optimizing world economy in Nordhaus (1994) suggest that the social costs of doing much today and in the near future to reduce the rate of global warming would far exceed the benefits: opti-mal carbon taxes in Nordhaus' simulations are quite low.

Why is this? There are two interrelated reasons. First, Nordhaus' most favored specification has it that total factor productivity increases over time (although at a declining rate—the rate halving every seventy years). This assumption, among others, implies that the effect of global warming on world output is small: a doubling of carbon dioxide (CO_2) concentration (corresponding to something like a three-degree Celsius increase in average global temperature) would result in a mere 1.33% loss in world output of goods and services (Nordhaus 1994, 51). Secondly, social rates of discount in Nordhaus' optimizing world economy are positive and nonnegligible throughout, and they make the small losses in world per capita consumption in the distant future due to global warming look really small today.[19]

The first of Nordhaus' assumptions mentioned earlier is followed with little questioning by modern growth theorists, but we doubt if it is prudent to postulate everlasting increases in total factor productivity, let alone in per capita output. To do so would be to place an enormous burden of proof on an experience that is not much more than a few hundred years old. Extrapolation into the past is a sobering exercise: over the long haul (say, a few thousand years), the rate of growth of per capita income has not been much more than zero.

Then, there are scientific reasons why we should be wary of relying on unspecified technological progress that is postulated to overcome ecological constraints. But the limits to growth are not so much that we will run out of resources as that the vast array of ecological services we rely on are finite in scope. For these reasons, it is not unreasonable to assume no technological change when evaluating the long-term consequences of economic policies.

The second of Nordhaus's assumptions to which we have alluded is also standard. We do not know of any exercise in project evaluation that has used a zero, not to mention negative, rate of interest for discounting future flows of a project's income. But, are consumption rates of interest inevitably positive? As we will see below, standard models of economic growth have features built into them that make consumption interest rates positive. But, standard models are an inadequate vehicle for obtaining insights into social discount rates when production and consumption activities involve externalities that filter into the distant future through the accumulation of some "public bad." Since global warming is a prime example of such externalities, we will use it as a backdrop for our discussion.

Consider first a world economy in which project choice is seen as policy reform (see the first section of this paper).[20] Assume that the economy is otherwise laissez-faire. If global warming is expected to lead to declines in (weighted) global consumption over some extended period in the distant future, then from expression (8) we would conclude that, over this same extended period, consumption rates of interest could well be *negative*. Suppose, for example, that $\delta = 0.01$ per year and that global consumption would be expected to decline at 2% a year for a period beginning thirty years from now if emissions of greenhouse gases were to continue at their laissez-faire rates. If $\alpha(C_t) = 2.5$ in expression (8), the consumption rate of interest would be –0.04 per year from Year 30 until the end of the period in question. Long-lasting projects that contribute to further global warming would not look so good because, from our current viewpoint, future losses due to global warming would be *amplified*; they would not be reduced to negligible figures by the relentless application of positive discount rates.

But, what about an optimizing economy? Here, the Ramsey Rule, expression (9), comes into play and matters become more complex. In standard models of economic growth, the social rate of return on investment equals the private rate (there are no externalities), and the private rate equals the marginal productivity of capital. As the latter is positive, the left-hand side of expression (9) is positive. Since the consumption rate of interest (the right-hand side) equals this, it must be positive as well.

Matters would be different if production activities were to contribute to the accumulation of some "public bad." The social rate of return on investment would differ from its private rate; and so, the fact that the private rate is positive would not mean that the social rate is positive. Imagine, for example, that laissez-faire policies in the past have resulted in the accumulation of a large stock of the public bad (for example, CO_2 concentration). Assume that the government now wants to pursue an optimal economic policy. If emissions are a by-product of production, one way to lower emissions would be to reduce output.[21] And one way to reduce output would be to leave idle some of the existing stock of physical capital. However, if it is optimal to do this for a while, then, during that while there would be no sense in accumulating capital. This is another way of saying that gross investment in physical capital should be zero, which, in turn, is another way of saying that all output ought to be consumed. At the margin, the social value of consumption then would not equal the social value of investment. So, the accounting price of consumption would differ from the accounting price of investment. It is obvious also that, if capacity were left idle, the social rate of return on investment would be zero. This means that if output or investment is numeraire, the social rate of discount would be zero. We will confirm this in the context of a formal model.

A NOT-TOO-FAR-FETCHED MODEL OF GLOBAL WARMING TO ILLUSTRATE THAT SOCIAL DISCOUNT RATES CAN BE ZERO EVEN IN AN OPTIMIZING WORLD

The model economy we will consider is a simple generalization of Ramsey (1928) and a special case of Nordhaus (1994).[22]

The Basic Model

Population is constant; there is no technological change; and there is no uncertainty.[23] Let K denote the quantity of physical capital in existence and the quantity used in production. So,

$$\widetilde{K} \le K \tag{13}$$

Gross output, Y, is

$$Y = \sigma\widetilde{K}e^{-\pi E} \tag{14}$$

where $\sigma, \pi > 0$, and E is the stock of a public bad (for example, CO_2 concentration).[24]

Capital used in production depreciates at a constant rate, ε (> 0). To make the points we would like to raise in a forceful manner, we take it that idle capital does not depreciate. Therefore, if C denotes aggregate consumption, accumulation of physical capital is governed by

$$\frac{dK}{dt} = \sigma\widetilde{K}e^{-\pi E} - C - \varepsilon\widetilde{K} \tag{15}$$

We assume capital cannot be consumed. So, gross investment must be nonnegative. This means,

$$\sigma\widetilde{K}e^{-\pi E} \ge C \tag{16}$$

In order to present the simplest possible model of the problem in hand, we will suppose that emissions of the public bad are a proportion, β, of current output, and that the only way emissions can be lowered is by reducing output. In short, β is the emission-output ratio.[25] The public bad is assumed to depreciate at a percentage rate, γ (> 0).[26] So we have

$$\frac{dE}{dt} = \sigma\beta\widetilde{K}e^{-\pi E} - \gamma E \tag{17}$$

Thus far, the physical model. We will now study production and consumption activities in two institutions: the laissez-faire economy and the optimal economy.

The Laissez-Faire Economy

There is a continuum of identical households distributed uniformly over the unit interval. Households are infinitely lived. The representative household's intertemporal utility function is

$$\int_0^\infty e^{-\delta t} U(C) dt \qquad (18)$$

where $\delta > 0$ and $U(C)$ is an increasing, strictly concave function.

Households own identical amounts of physical capital. As there is no environmental policy in the laissez-faire economy, the market price of E is zero: it is a pure public bad. The private rate of return on investment is, therefore, $\sigma e^{-\pi E}$. Moreover, $\widetilde{K} = K$.

A *rational expectations equilibrium* of the laissez-faire economy is a time path of C, K, E, and Y, such that it is the consequence of the following maximization problem:

Choose C to maximize equation (18), subject to conditions (15)–(17) being satisfied with rational expectations, and $\widetilde{K} = K$; with K_0 and E_0 as the initial values of the two stock variables. (19)

Our treatment will be informal. Moreover, we will confine ourselves to *stationary* rational expectations equilibriums. Let P be the spot price of consumption in terms of utility numeraire. It is a routine matter to confirm that the stationary point(s) must satisfy the conditions:

$$\sigma K e^{-\pi E} = C + \varepsilon K I \qquad (20)$$

$$\sigma \beta K e^{-\pi E} = \gamma E \qquad (21)$$

$$U'(C) = P \qquad (22)$$

$$\sigma e^{-\pi E} = \delta + \varepsilon \qquad (23)$$

$$\sigma K e^{-\pi E} = Y \qquad (24)$$

Equations (20)–(24) are five in number, and there are five unknowns: C, K, E, Y, and P. Assume $\sigma > \delta + \varepsilon$ (that is, the economy is productive). It is then immediate that the unique stationary value of E (call it E^{**}) is

$$E^{**} = \pi^{-1} \log [\sigma/(\delta + \varepsilon)] \qquad (25)$$

And so forth. Let C^{**}, K^{**}, Y^{**}, and P^{**} denote the stationary values of the remaining variables. We wish to compare them with their optimal stationary values. We turn to this.

The Optimal Economy

The public authority respects household preferences. Its maximizing problem is

Choose C to maximize equation (18), subject to conditions
(13)–(17), with K_0 and E_0 as initial values of the two stocks.   (26)

Let Q and S denote the auxiliary variables associated with equations
(15) and (17), respectively. If utility is numeraire, Q is the (spot) accounting price of investment, and S is the (spot) accounting price of environmental pollution. We will confirm that $Q > 0$ and $S < 0$.

The present-value Hamiltonian, H_0, of expression (26) can now be
expressed as

$$H_0 = e^{-\delta t}U(C) + e^{-\delta t}Q(\sigma\widetilde{K}e^{-\pi E} - C - \varepsilon\widetilde{K}) + e^{-\delta t}S(\sigma\beta\widetilde{K}e^{-\pi E} - \gamma E) +$$
$$e^{-\delta t}M(K - \widetilde{K}) + e^{-\delta t}N(\sigma\widetilde{K}e^{-\pi E} - C) \tag{27}$$

where

$$M \geq 0, \text{ and } M(K - \widetilde{K}) = 0 \text{ with complementary slackness} \tag{28a}$$

and

$$N \geq 0 \text{ and } N(\sigma\widetilde{K}e^{-\pi E} - C) = 0 \text{ with complementary slackness.} \tag{28b}$$

Routine calculations show that the optimal policy must satisfy the following conditions:

$$U'(C) = Q + N \tag{29}$$

$$\sigma e^{-\pi E}(Q + \beta S + N) = M + \varepsilon Q \tag{30}$$

$$(dQ/dt)/Q = \delta - M/Q \tag{31}$$

and

$$(dS/dt)/S = \delta + \sigma\pi\widetilde{K}e^{-\pi E}[(Q/S) + \beta + (N/S)] + \gamma \tag{32}$$

From conditions (28a) and (28b), we can conclude that if $M = 0$, then
$N > 0$. Notice, too, that when $\widetilde{K} < K$, equation (31) reduces to

$$dQ/dt = \delta Q \tag{33}$$

So, *if investment or output is numeraire, the social rate of discount is zero
whenever it is optimal to hold idle capacity.* Notice as well that when $N > 0$
(that is, it is optimal to consume all output), consumption and investment

have different accounting prices. From equation (29), we see that, relative to utility, the spot price of consumption is $(Q + N)$, which is greater than Q.

What is *net national product* (NNP) along the optimal program? NNP is the linearized Hamiltonian (Dasgupta and Mäler 1991; Mäler 1991). Denote the current value of NNP by Z. From equation (27), we conclude that, if consumption is numeraire,

$$Z = C + [Q/(Q + N)]dK/dt + [S/(Q + N)]dE/dt \qquad (34)$$

Macroeconomic programs consist of projects; and projects, taken together, make a macroeconomic program, for recall that a project is a perturbation to a macroeconomic program. Write $I = dK/dt$ and $J = dE/dt$. We will call any feasible, one-period perturbation, (dC, dI, dJ), to a macroeconomic program an *elementary project*. All feasible investment projects can be viewed as a compound of elementary projects. In the first section of this paper, we recalled that accounting prices can be used for sustaining an optimal program in a decentralized environment. In the present context, this means that small investment projects could be decomposed into their constituent, elementary projects and evaluated on the basis of a repeated use of equation (32) as the criterion of choice. Alternatively (and equivalently), we could avoid decomposing the projects by evaluating them directly on the basis of their contribution to the present discounted value of the flow of Z. Either way, the set of projects that would be chosen would comprise the optimal program. The marginal project would contribute nothing to NNP.

At a stationary point of the optimal program, $\widetilde{K} = K$ and $Y > C$. So, from conditions (28) and equations (20)–(21) and (29)–(31), we may conclude that the stationary values must satisfy the conditions

$$\sigma K e^{-\pi E} = C + \varepsilon K \qquad (35)$$

$$\sigma \beta K e^{-\pi E} = \gamma E \qquad (36)$$

$$U'(C) = Q \qquad (37)$$

$$\sigma e^{-\pi E}(Q + \beta S) = M + \varepsilon Q \qquad (38)$$

$$\delta = M/Q \qquad (39)$$

$$\delta + \sigma \pi K e^{-\pi E}[(Q/S) + \beta] + \gamma = 0 \qquad (40)$$

$$\sigma K e^{-\pi E} = Y \qquad (41)$$

Equations (35)–(41) are seven in number, and there are seven unknowns, Q, S, C, K, E, Y, and M. Routine manipulations with them yields

$$\sigma(\delta + \gamma)e^{-\pi E} = (\delta + \varepsilon)\pi\gamma E + (\delta + \varepsilon)(\delta + \gamma) \qquad (42)$$

Since $\sigma > (\delta + \varepsilon)$, equation (42) has a unique solution. Call it E^*. Write $X \equiv Q/S$. From equations (35)–(41) it is an easy matter to confirm that the stationary value of X (call it X^*) is

$$X^* = (\delta e^{\pi E^*} - \sigma)/\sigma\beta < 0$$

And so forth for the rest of the variables. Let C^*, K^*, Y^*, Q^*, S^* and M^* denote the unique stationary values of the remaining variables. The social rate of discount in the stationary state is δ, independent of numeraire.

A Comparison of Two Economies

On using equations (25) and (41), we conclude that

$$E^{**} > E^*, K^{**} > K^*, \text{ and } Y^{**} > Y^* \qquad (43)$$

Thus, in the long run, *the laissez-faire economy, compared with the optimizing economy, suffers from greater pollution, has a larger stock of physical capital, and produces more output.* In short, the laissez-faire economy is too large: it should cut down its economic activities.

What of consumption though? When comparison is limited to stationary states, does the laissez-faire economy consume too much or too little? The answer is not unambiguous. However, it is easy to show that, *if ε is "small," then $C^{**} > C^*$; or, in the long run, consumption level in the laissez-faire economy is too high.*

Suppose, instead, that the economy has been run along laissez-faire lines for a long while. The government now wants to manage it optimally. If the laissez-faire economy had tracked a rational-expectations equilibrium path, the initial values of the two state variables in expression (26) would be K^{**} and E^{**}. But, the idea of a rational-expectations equilibrium of a laissez-faire economy appears unreasonable to many economists. If it were to be dispensed with as a descriptive construct, there would be no natural initial values of K and E in expression (26): we could entertain the possibility that both are arbitrarily large.

Since the optimal economy transits to lower values of the two stocks (K^* and E^*), we would expect an initial phase when capacity is not used in full and when all output is consumed. During this phase, the social rate of discount (in investment numeraire) would be zero. It is only when the stocks of both physical capital and environmental pollution are decumulated sufficiently that full capacity would be optimal.

One can prove this for the case, $K_0 \gg K^*$ and $E_0 > E^*$ in expression (26).[27] But, we have been unable to prove that there is a transient phase like this when the initial values are K^{**} and E^{**}; that is, we have been unable to piece together a complete narrative of phases. But, it is a possibility that simulations with the model would uncover. This is the next task.

CONCLUSIONS

This paper has been about the logic underlying social discount rates. We have argued that these rates are not ethical raw material but are derived from the more fundamental notion of justice among generations. A number of approaches to the concept of intergenerational justice were discussed, and it was argued that the most compelling formulation available to us is the one that has long been in use among economists, namely, the Ramsey-Koopmans theory. This theory advocates that investment projects having long-run effects should be subjected to the same conceptual treatment as those that affect only the near future. We have shown that social discount rates depend on the numeraire, and that methods of estimating them depend on the institutional setting within which social benefit-cost analysis is assumed to be undertaken. We have also shown that it is incorrect to advocate project-specific discount rates as a way of conserving environmental resources.

Social discount rates have universally been taken to be positive, on the grounds that the rate of return on investment is positive. But, if consumption and production activities give rise to environmental pollution as a by-product, the social rate of return on investment could be zero even when the private rate is positive; at the very least, the social rate would be lower than the private rate. The current practice among most global energy modelers of relying exclusively on (risk-free) market rates of return for estimating optimal carbon taxes is conceptually faulty. In the context of a formal model of environmental pollution, we have shown how, even along an optimal program, social rates of discount can be zero. We also demonstrated that in certain institutional settings, social discount rates can be negative.

ACKNOWLEDGEMENTS

We are most grateful to Kenneth Arrow, James Mirrlees, and V. Kerry Smith for their helpful comments.

ENDNOTES

[1]We are, of course, assuming that an optimum exists.

[2]The circumstances are those in which the Kuhn-Tucker theorem holds. Accounting prices are sometimes called "shadow prices" and also, by the technocratically minded, "Lagrange multipliers." In what follows, public policy choice will be interpreted as choice over investment projects.

[3]Arrow and others (1996) provide a summary of the various guidelines we possess on how social discount rates can be estimated from observable data.

[4]See Uzawa (1958) and Arrow and Hurwicz (1958) for a formal demonstration; and see Dasgupta, Marglin, and Sen (1972) and Ahmad and Stern (1990) for the development of practical methods for project evaluation and policy reform based on the finding.

[5]Other well-known and instructive models of the economics of global warming are Cline (1992), Manne and Richels (1992), and Peck and Teisberg (1992).

[6]We will use the terms "well-being," "welfare," and "utility" interchangeably here.

[7]There is no discounting if $\phi = 1$.

[8]Equation (5) reduces to equation (3) if $T = \infty$.

[9]This section is taken from Dasgupta (1994) and Dasgupta and Mäler (1995).

[10]Ethical foundations of population policies have been explored in Dasgupta (1969, 1994).

[11]To concentrate on intergenerational matters, we are therefore ignoring intragenerational distributional issues here.

[12]Indeed, no ecologist we know thinks that a population of some ten billion (which is a reasonable projection for world population in the year 2050) can support itself indefinitely at the standard of living of today's representative West European.

[13]Unlike uniform boundedness of Γ_C, this is not a requirement dictated by ecology.

[14]This is not strictly true, since Koopmans assumed constant population. But his analysis extends to the present case. Moreover, Koopmans worked with discrete time. In Koopmans (1972), the ethical axioms are imposed directly on Γ_C, a considerable generalization.

[15]See, for example, Arrow and Kurz (1970). $U'(C_t)$ is the accounting price of consumption at date t in terms of utility at t. So, $\exp(-\delta t)U'(C_t)$ is its present-value price in terms of utility at $t = 0$. The percentage rate of decline of this expression is $\rho(C_t)$.

[16]This function is unbounded below and so violates the Koopmans axioms.

[17]Beltratti, Chichilnisky, and Heal (1995); Chichilnisky (1994); and Radner (1967) provide alternative rationales for this when U is bounded.

[18]Schelling (1992) and Ehrlich and Ehrlich (1996) provide excellent summaries of what we know and what we do not know.

[19]The rate is 5.9% per year in 1995 and declines to about 4.4% per year in 2075, as growth in per capita world output slows in the second half of the next century (Nordhaus 1994, 91).

[20]This paragraph is taken from Dasgupta and Mäler (1995, 2401).

[21]Others would be to treat emissions before they disperse (for example, the use of stack-gas scrubbers for removing the sulfur dioxide produced when coal is burned), use cleaner, but more expensive technologies (for example, the use of clean energy), and clean up the pollution after it has been emitted (for example, artificially aerate eutrophied bodies of water, sequester additional CO_2 from the atmosphere by planting trees, and so forth). Dasgupta (1982, Chap. 8) analyzes a model of pollution containing all these options.

[22]But, with a difference: Nordhaus does not allow for the possibility that the optimal economy can have idle capacity.

[23]Variables will be represented by upper-case letters and constants by lower-case ones. Therefore, we may as well suppress the time subscript from the former.

[24]A major weakness of this model of global warming, and, indeed, all models with which we are familiar, is that the dynamic processes underlying them display no irreversibilities. Thus, for example, catastrophes are not a possibility in climate models. In other words, there are no naturally occurring bifurcations.

A simple formulation would have it that it is *changes* in the level of the public bad that are bad for production. A natural way of formulating this is to write $Y = \sigma \exp(-\pi \, dE/dt)$. But, our aim here is to make a number of analytical points, not to simulate the world. So, we do not try to build in such complications.

[25]In their article on optimal environmental taxation, Ulph and Ulph (1994), quite rightly, relate emissions (of CO_2) to the use of fossil fuels in production, not to production itself.

[26]Thus, the rate of sequestration is not determined within the model. Under current conditions, the mean residence time of CO_2 in the atmosphere is a century or more. This suggests $\gamma \leq 0.01$ per year.

[27]The intuition is that, as the inherited stock of physical capital is "very" large, output at full capacity is very large and, so, adds to the stock of pollution. Holding idle capacity and simultaneously consuming all output are a way of reducing the stocks of both types of capital.

REFERENCES

Ahmad, E., and N. Stern. 1990. *The Theory and Practice of Tax Reform for Developing Countries.* Cambridge: Cambridge University.

Arrow, K. J. 1973. Rawls' Principle of Just Savings. *Swedish Journal of Economics* 75(4): 323–35.

Arrow, K. J., and A. C. Fisher. 1974. Preservation, Uncertainty, and Irreversibility. *Quarterly Journal of Economics* 88(2): 312–19.

Arrow, K. J., and L. Hurwicz. 1958. Gradient Method for Concave Programming, III: Further Global Results and Applications to Resource Allocation. In K. J. Arrow, L. Hurwicz, and H. Uzawa (eds.), *Studies in Linear and Non-Linear Programming*. Stanford, California: Stanford University Press, 133–45.

Arrow, K. J., and M. Kurz. 1970. *Public Investment, the Rate of Return, and Optimal Fiscal Policy*. Baltimore: Johns Hopkins University Press.

Arrow, K. J., and others. 1996. Intertemporal Equity, Discounting, and Economic Efficiency. In J. P. Bruce, H. Lee, and E. F. Haites (eds.), *Climate Change 1995: Economic and Social Dimensions of Climate Change*. Contribution of Working Group III to the Second Assessment Report of the Intergovernmental Panel on Climate Change. Cambridge: Cambridge University Press.

Barro, R., and G. Becker. 1989. Fertility Choice in a Model of Economic Growth. *Econometrica* 57(2): 481–501.

Barro, R., and X. Sala-i-Martin. 1995. *Economic Growth*. New York: McGraw-Hill.

Beltratti, A., G. Chichilnisky, and G. Heal. 1995. Sustainable Growth and the Green Golden Rule. In I. Goldin and L. A. Winters (eds.), *The Economics of Sustainable Development*. Cambridge: Cambridge University Press, 147–74.

Bewley, T. 1989. *Market Innovation and Entrepreneurship: A Knightian View*. Cowles Foundation Discussion Paper No. 905. New Haven, Connecticut: Yale University.

Chakravarty, S. 1969. *Capital and Development Planning*. Cambridge, Massachusetts: MIT Press.

Chichilnisky, G. 1994. Intergenerational Equity and Sustainable Development. New York: Department of Economics, Columbia University. Mimeographed.

Cline, W. R. 1992. *The Economics of Global Warming*. Washington, D.C.: Institute for International Economics.

Cowen, T., and D. Parfit. 1992. Against the Social Discount Rate. In P. Laslett and J. S. Fishkin (eds.), *Justice Between Age Groups and Generations*. New Haven, Connecticut: Yale University Press, 144–61.

Daly, H. E., and J. B. Cobb. 1991. *For the Common Good: Redirecting the Economy Towards Community, the Environment, and a Sustainable Future*. London: Greenprint.

Dasgupta, P. 1969. On the Concept of Optimum Population. *Review of Economic Studies* 36(3): 294–318.

———. 1974. On Some Alternative Criteria for Justice Between Generations. *Journal of Public Economics* 3(4): 405–23.

———. 1982. *The Control of Resources*. Cambridge, Massachusetts: Harvard University Press.

———. 1994. Saving and Fertility: Ethical Issues. *Philosophy and Public Affairs* 23(2): 99–127.

————. 1996. On Discounting One's Own Future and That of Future Generations. Cambridge: Faculty of Economics, Cambridge University. Mimeographed.

Dasgupta, P., and G. M. Heal. 1979. *Economic Theory and Exhaustible Resources.* Cambridge: Cambridge University Press.

Dasgupta, P., and K.-G. Mäler. 1991. *The Environment and Emerging Development Issues.* Proceedings of the World Bank Annual Conference on Development Economics 1990. Supplement to the *World Bank Economic Review* and the *World Bank Research Observer.* Washington, D.C.: World Bank, 101–32.

————. 1995. Poverty, Institutions, and the Environmental Resource-Base. In J. Behrman and T. N. Srinivasan (eds.), *Handbook of Development Economics.* Vol. IIIA. Amsterdam: North Holland, 2371–2463.

Dasgupta, P., S. Marglin, and A. Sen. 1972. *Guidelines for Project Evaluation.* New York: United Nations.

Ehrlich, P. R., and A. H. Ehrlich. 1996. *Betrayal of Science and Reason.* Washington, D.C.: Island Press/Shearwater Books.

Henry, C. 1974. Investment Decisions under Uncertainty: The Irreversibility Effect. *American Economic Review* 64(6): 1006–12.

Houghton, J. T., ed. 1996. *Climate Change 1995: The Science of Climate Change.* Contribution of Working Group I to the Second Assessment Report of the Intergovernmental Panel on Climate Change. Cambridge: Cambridge University Press.

Koopmans, T. C. 1960. Stationary Ordinal Utility and Impatience. *Econometrica* 28(2): 287–309.

————. 1972. Representation of Preference Orderings over Time. In C. B. McGuire and R. Radner (eds.), *Decision and Organization.* Amsterdam: North Holland, 79–101.

Lind, R. C., ed. 1982. *Discounting for Time and Risk in Energy Planning.* Baltimore: Johns Hopkins University Press.

Little, I. M. D., and J. A. Mirrlees. 1974. *Project Appraisal and Planning for Developing Countries.* London: Heinemann.

Mäler, K.-G. 1991. National Accounting and Environmental Resources. *Environment and Resource Economics* 1(1): 1–27.

Manne, A. S., and R. Richels. 1992. *Buying Greenhouse Insurance: The Economic Costs of CO_2 Emissions Limits.* Cambridge, Massachusetts: MIT Press.

Nordhaus, W. D. 1977. Economic Growth and Climate: The Carbon Dioxide Problem. *American Economic Review* 67 (Papers and Proceedings): 341–46.

————. 1994. *Managing the Global Commons: The Economics of Climate Change.* Cambridge, Massachusetts: MIT Press.

Nordhaus, W. D., and Z. Yang. 1996. A Regional Dynamic General-Equilibrium Model of Alternative Climate-Change Strategies. *American Economic Review* 86(4): 741–65.

Parfit, D. 1984. *Reasons and Persons.* Oxford: Oxford University Press.

Peck, S. C., and T. J. Teisberg. 1992. CETA: A Model for Carbon Emissions Trajectory Assessment. *Energy Journal* 13(1): 55–77.

Phelps, E. S., and R. Pollak. 1968. Second-Best National Savings and Game Equilibrium Growth. *Review of Economic Studies* 35(2): 185–99.

Radner, R. 1967. Efficiency Prices for Infinite Horizon Production Programmes. *Review of Economic Studies* 34(1): 51–66.

Ramsey, F. 1928. A Mathematical Theory of Saving. *Economic Journal* 38(4): 543–59.

Rawls, J. 1972. *A Theory of Justice.* Oxford: Clarendon Press.

Romer, D. 1996. *Advanced Macroeconomics.* New York: McGraw-Hill.

Schelling, T. C. 1992. Some Economics of Global Warming. *American Economic Review* 82(1): 1–14.

———. 1995. Intergenerational Discounting. *Energy Policy* 23(4–5): 395–401.

Solow, R. M. 1974a. The Economics of Resources, or the Resources of Economics. *American Economic Review* 64 (Papers and Proceedings): 1–21.

———. 1974b. Intergenerational Equity and Exhaustible Resources. *Review of Economic Studies* 41 (Symposium on the Economics of Exhaustible Resources): 29–45.

Ulph, A., and D. Ulph. 1994. The Optimal Time Path of a Carbon Tax. *Oxford Economic Papers* 46 (Special Issue on Environmental Economics): 857–69.

Uzawa, H. 1958. Gradient Method for Concave Programming, II: Global Stability in the Strictly Concave Case. In K. J. Arrow, L. Hurwicz, and H. Uzawa (eds.), *Studies in Linear and Non-Linear Programming.* Stanford, California: Stanford University Press, 127–32.

Vitousek, P., and others. 1986. Human Appropriation of the Products of Photosynthesis. *BioScience* 36: 368–73.

8

Substitution and Social Discount Rates

Comments on Dasgupta, Mäler, and Barrett

V. Kerry Smith

Our current reconsideration of the present value criterion for public choices involving very long time horizons or the *deep future* is at least partially motivated by a puzzle. This puzzle follows from a dissatisfaction with the conclusions from standard benefit-cost techniques. In these cases we find *negative* values for the discounted net benefits from actions intended to respond to what is usually a long-term, large-scale problem that many people—policy analysts, policymakers, and the lay public—feel needs to be addressed. Our economic evaluation of these questions suggests the opposite conclusion.

Some economists and philosophers have been observing for some time that this outcome should not be surprising.[1] For them, economic analysis does not inform these decisions. Most economists have responded to the puzzle differently. They suggest what is needed involves a renewed consideration of the relevance of a present value criterion and in particular a special focus on the size of the discount rate used in these calculations.

The problems falling in this group are complex for a number of reasons. Some examples illustrate why. Three frequently cited cases are:

- disposal of commercial nuclear waste,
- decommissioning and ultimate disposal of weapon systems designed for mass destruction (as well as the effluents generated in making them), and

V. KERRY SMITH is Arts and Sciences Professor of Environmental Economics, Duke University, and Resources for the Future University Fellow.

- reductions in the rate of accumulation of the stock pollutants associated with climate change and thinning of the ozone layer.

In each case we have very incomplete (and often highly uncertain) knowledge about the future consequences of the choice options available. Some of the effects of bad choices would be catastrophic and irreversible. Thus, the problems also evoke strong beliefs about what constitutes ethical behavior on the part of the current generation in relationship to the future.

The papers is this volume offer a variety of explanations for special concern about these types of questions. Implicitly they ask whether this angst is evidence of a cognitive failure of most people to comprehend the full implications of the compounding effects of discounting; a reflection of the failure of the rational economic model as a basis for informing these decisions; an indication of the inappropriateness of the present value criterion of benefit-cost analysis for this class of problems; or simply a matter of selecting a different social rate of discount. This volume offers the *core* arguments of the economists whose work has collectively defined what the rest of us think we know about the practice of discounting and the selection of the social rate of discount. The arguments of Dasgupta, Mäler, and Barrett (DM&B) in Chapter 7 are especially fundamental. They expose a central tenet in the simplifications that underlie how economic models evaluate actions assumed to alter a society's optimal growth program.

BACKGROUND FOR DM&B

To appreciate the DM&B strategy for analyzing these questions and to comment on the broader relevance of their conclusions, I need to highlight a few ingredients of their models. First, they accept Koopmans' (1972) arguments as providing a defensible ethical basis for a present value criterion. Second, they acknowledge the potential importance of irreversibilities in conditioning decision criteria *but* abstract from this dimension of the problem. Third, and most important, they introduce natural capital into the social "choice set." Decisions about this natural capital are indirect because its status changes through impact experienced "by default" under their laissez-faire regime and "by design" under an optimal program.

They find that it is possible, within the format of their model, to call for periods where it would be optimal for society to halt growth in the productive capital stock. This conclusion implies that during these periods the implied rate of discount (interpreted as a marginal product of capital) would be zero (or even negative)! Close inspection of their framework might lead commentators to suggest that this result, while intriguing, is not surprising. The model gives society no alternative if for some reason the initial conditions defining the starting point for an optimal program imply there has been too much depletion of natural capital (or equivalently, too much accumulation of the stock pollutant E). The model allows only one option to adjust—reduce current production and wait for the regenerative process of natural capital $(-\gamma E)$ to restore itself.

If the framework is altered in a way that introduces some form of "produced restoration" (or, equivalently, allows society to "throw money" at the problem directly rather than indirectly), then we are back to balancing the returns to capital in its different uses and a positive discount rate. From my perspective, the issues Dasgupta, Mäler, and Barrett pose are fundamental to the role of economic analysis in informing these choices and a set of comments that focuses on such a "quick fix" adaptation to their model would miss them completely.

IMPLICATIONS OF DM&B

The striking DM&B observation, that optimal behavior might require a zero social rate of discount, is not, in my view, the most fundamental implication of their analysis. The simple models that relate the dichotomy underlying the *prescriptive*, or right, side of equation (1) below (that is, a focus on ethical issues and the objective function used to define society's goals for an optimal program) and *descriptive*, or left, side of equation (1) (that is, a focus on the productivity of capital) achieve this distillation of the issues by imposing simplified substitution assumptions on their model of economic activities in relationship to the natural environment. These assumptions ultimately control the trade-offs defining what is important about all resource allocations.

$$F_{K_t} = \delta + \alpha(C_t) \cdot \left(\frac{\dot{C}_t}{C_t} \right) \qquad (1)$$

where the symbols correspond to those in DM&B.

Introducing natural capital (or their stock of pollutant E) requires that the conditions for an optimal program be modified so that our descriptive term (F_K) is adjusted to reflect the social costs of producing output (that is, in terms of the deterioration of the natural capital). This effect also changes over time and *with the initial conditions at the outset of an optimal program*. This adjustment appears to be an "objective" or technical correction (an output adjustment) because of how accumulated pollution (E) is assumed to impact people (through their ability to produce output). This conclusion is most easily recognized by developing the equivalent of equation (1) for their model with natural capital, as in equation (2) below

$$F_{K_t} + \frac{\lambda_{2t}}{\lambda_{1t}} \sigma \beta e^{-\pi E_t} = \delta + \alpha(C_t) \cdot \left(\frac{\dot{C}_t}{C_t} \right) \tag{2}$$

where λ_{1t}, λ_{2t} are the co-state variables for the constraints associated with the accumulation of produced capital and the degradation of natural capital respectively ($\lambda_{1t} > 0$ and $\lambda_{2t} < 0$). The second term on the left side of equation (2) *reduces* the marginal product of capital to reflect its environmental costs in terms of the difficulties in producing future output. These difficulties arise because society is using up natural capital as it accumulates the stock pollutant E. If we were to assume it affected the specification for societal well-being directly, the results would be quite different and the focus would be prescriptive.[2] These specifications are but two of the many possibilities. Because the services provided by environmental resources to people are usually available outside markets, we learn little about their relevance from market prices. DM&B's analysis suggests their role can be crucial. This is especially true if the policy choice involves them directly.

A NEW VIEW OF SUBSTITUTION

Concern about the long-term consequences of people's uses of natural and environmental resources is certainly not new. More than forty years ago, such concern motivated the foundation of Resources for the Future (RFF), one of the sponsors of the conference leading to this volume. After careful empirical analysis, Barnett and Morse (1963) concluded one of RFF's first major research efforts by noting that materials (that is, natural resources) scarcity had been avoided because technical change had served as the "renewing resource," offering opportunities to the nimble to respond. A little more than ten years later, another look at the issue suggested that substitution between produced capital and natural resources, technical change, and demand-based substitutions can potentially mitigate (or eliminate) the prospects for natural resource scarcity.[3] Subsequent work has repeated these lessons. In all cases the authors have also identified one important reason for anxiety arising from the treatment of environmental resources. What was argued was that the effects of these resources may be important but typically are not considered. They are generally available outside markets and thus do not get "counted" in the conventional economic models.

One of the most important implications of the DM&B paper extends beyond the issues in selecting a social rate of discount to this earlier context. DM&B's model highlights how an economy makes substitutions between produced and environmental capital. A narrow definition of what determines observed substitutions among inputs to production activities would focus exclusively on their production function, finding a specification where the interrelationship between natural capital and the environment changes as pollutant E accumulates.[4] However, this view is incomplete.

Along the lines of an optimal program, we must consider how the natural system constrains feasible substitutions (in DM&B's case through the description of the depreciation rate for the stock pollutant). Both technology and the environmental system determine what will be the "feasible substitutions." Conclusions about appropriate value (or function) to describe the social rate of discount are not robust to how the model characterizes the factors relevant to the produced/environmental capital substitution along an optimal program.

A BOTTOM LINE FOR THE SOCIAL RATE OF DISCOUNT

The present value puzzle for complex, *deep future* problems will not be reconciled by simple (and universal) adjustments to the social rate of discount. DM&B's analysis has shown that the details of each problem matter. Moreover, in the time horizon relevant to most of these decisions, we will not know the answers to questions about how to characterize the ways environmental resources contribute to economic activities and people's well-being. Consequently, my bottom-line conclusion is that in selecting a social rate of discount we should use a real, risk-free rate of return, provided we are also prepared to use two other sets of information in the economic analysis intended to inform these types of decisions.

The first of these recognizes the sensitivity of such rates of return to the types of economic and environmental resources that sustain an optimal growth program. This is particularly true for decisions with irreversible consequences. Analysis must focus on characterizing the possibilities with these alternatives (especially those considered to be in the policy choice set) and, to the extent feasible, their relative plausibility.

In most cases intervention is motivated by concern over the laissez-faire outcomes. With the uncertainty that surrounds all aspects of these problems, public action is really intended to provide "insurance" against the bad outcomes.[5] It is rarely conceived as fixing the problem, either because the problem itself may ultimately prove to be less important, or alternatively, because the available actions may have appreciable unintended consequences. As Kopp and Portney suggest in Chapter 9, a decision to take action necessarily imposes costs on the current generation (effectively paying for the insurance through the resources devoted to the policy). As a result, the preferences of this generation *should be* a part of the information considered, and information about these preferences comprise the second set of information necessary to inform these choices. While there may well be reasons to suggest that measures of these preferences should not be the decisive factor, it is also true that they cannot be ignored. Choices left to an elite that either conducts or uses the analysis of these types of problems are no more sustainable than a policy that ignores the long-term environmental consequences of current economic activities.

ACKNOWLEDGEMENTS

Partial support for this research was provided by NOAA grant #NA46GPO466.

ENDNOTES

[1]A good summary of these arguments can be found in Norton (1995) where he proposes an environmental risk decision square plotting the magnitude of the impact on one axis and the degree of irreversibility on the other. Those decisions that had largest impact and with irreversible consequences would be decided outside the conventional economic paradigm.

[2]For a discussion of these possibilities see Kamien and Schwartz (1982) and Heal (1982). Kamien and Schwartz offer a parallel conclusion to DM&B for a somewhat more general production function but without the key regeneration effect of the environmental capital.

[3]A brief summary of the issues identified in this second round of research in relationship to the early Barnett-Morse work is in Smith and Krutilla (1984).

[4]The Allen elasticity of substitution (σ^{AES}) between produced capital and the implicit absorption capacity of environmental capital, measured through E, for the DM&B production function is given as:

$$\sigma^{AES} = 1 - \left(\frac{1}{\pi E} \right)$$

Thus, as the stock pollutant is allowed to become small, the services of produced and environmental capital would be complementary. This relationship changes as

E accumulates and, in fact, by this measure substitution would seem relatively smooth at high levels of E. Of course, description of the model indicates how misleading this index is for what might be termed substitution along an optimal program.

[5]Framing the issue in this way uses the original Arrow-Fisher (1974) insight, recognizing that delaying irreversible decisions thereby allows time to learn more about their potential consequences. Hanemann (1989) demonstrates that their quasi-option value corresponds to the conditional expected value of the information acquired from delay. Fisher and Hanemann (1986) discuss practical methods for measures of such benefits and, recently, Albers, Fisher, and Hanemann (1996) demonstrate how they would be used.

REFERENCES

Albers, Heidi, Anthony Fisher, and W. Michael Hanemann. 1996. Valuation and Management of Tropical Forests: Implications of Uncertainty and Irreversibility. *Environmental and Resource Economics* 8: 39–61.

Arrow, Kenneth J., and A. C. Fisher. 1974. Environmental Preservation, Uncertainty, and Irreversibility. *Quarterly Journal of Economics* 88(May): 312–19.

Barnett, Harold T., and Chandler Morse. 1963. *Scarcity and Growth: The Economics of Natural Resource Availability.* Baltimore: Johns Hopkins University.

Fisher, A. C., and W. M. Hanemann. 1986. Option Value and the Extinction of Species. In V. K. Smith (ed.), *Advances in Applied Micro-Economics.* Greenwich: JAI Press.

Hanemann, W. M. 1989. Information and the Concept of Option Value. *Journal of Environmental Economics and Management* 16(January): 23–37.

Heal, Geoffrey M. 1982. The Use of Common Property Resource. In V. Kerry Smith and John V. Krutilla (eds.), *Explorations in Natural Resource Economics.* Baltimore: Johns Hopkins University.

Kamien, Morton, and Nancy L. Schwartz. 1982. The Role of Common Property Resources in Optimal Planning Models With Exhaustible Resources. In V. Kerry Smith and John V. Krutilla (eds.), *Explorations in Natural Resource Economics.* Baltimore: Johns Hopkins University.

Koopmans, T. C. 1972. Representation of Preference Orderings Over Time. In C. B. McGuire and R. Radner (eds.), *Decision and Organization.* Amsterdam: North Holland.

Norton, Bryan G. 1995. Evaluating Ecosystem States: Two Competing Paradigms. *Ecological Economics* 14: 113–27.

Smith, V. Kerry, and John V. Krutilla. 1984. Economic Growth, Resource Availability and Environmental Quality. *American Economic Review, Proceedings* 74(May): 226–30.

9

Mock Referenda for Intergenerational Decisionmaking

Raymond J. Kopp and Paul R. Portney

Traditional applications of benefit-cost analysis make use of what we refer to as the "damage function and discounting" (or DFD) approach. This approach is well-suited to the analysis of projects for which the principal benefits and costs occur within, say, the next thirty to forty years. However, for projects with significant intergenerational consequences—that is, impacts that do not arise for hundreds of years or more—the DFD approach becomes almost intractable. We propose an alternative conception of benefit-cost analysis for intergenerational decisionmaking—the mock referendum—that is arguably more consistent with the tenets of modern welfare economics, more amenable to the analysis of long-term projects or policies, and consistent with political decisions that must be made if climate mitigation (or other long-term environmental protection) measures are to be taken.

THE DFD APPROACH

Virtually the entire literature on the application of benefit-cost analysis (BCA) to environmental issues is premised on the DFD Approach, which traditionally is composed of two distinct steps. First, the favorable and unfavorable effects of a proposed policy intervention at all future points in time are identified and expressed in dollar terms. (Subsumed here is

RAYMOND J. KOPP is Senior Fellow and PAUL R. PORTNEY is President and Senior Fellow at Resources for the Future.

the translation of the policy change into changes in environmental conditions—cleaner air, for instance—as well as the translation of the latter into
improved human health, enhanced visibility, reduced material damage
and other physical benefits.) Second, the time streams of future benefits
and costs are converted to present values using a single discount rate (or
a range of rates when a sensitivity analysis is included). It is difficult to
find even one benefit-cost assessment performed inside or outside government for a proposed environmental regulatory program that has not
adhered to the DFD approach.

Moreover, while the recent report of Working Group III of the Intergovernmental Panel on Climate Change (IPCC 1996) does contain some
discussion of alternative decisionmaking frameworks, the DFD approach
is by far the dominant paradigm, even if its primacy is implicit. Finally,
the pertinent chapter in that report—Intertemporal Equity, Discounting,
and Economic Efficiency—is clearly premised on this same approach.

For many environmental and other types of policy interventions, the
damage-function-and-discounting approach is a perfectly appropriate
means of analysis. In general, the DFD approach will be reasonable when
the principal benefits and costs associated with a project will occur
within, say, thirty or forty years. But for a handful of other, more "exotic"
proposed projects, the benefits and costs of which will be spread out over
many generations, the DFD approach becomes intractable for reasons
spelled out below. Examples of such projects or programs include proposed solutions to the storage of low- and high-level nuclear wastes (that
can remain highly radioactive for tens of thousands of years; see Kneese
1973), habitat protection for threatened and endangered species (that, if
they were to become extinct, would be forever lost to all future generations), and, of course, policies to slow or reverse the accumulation of carbon dioxide and other greenhouse gases in the atmosphere (the principal
benefits of which would not be felt for hundreds of years).[1]

This does *not* mean, however, that benefit-cost analysis has little to
contribute to the analysis of such problems. In fact, our purpose here is to
propose an alternative conception of BCA, which we refer to as a "mock
referendum," for application in cases where proposed policy interventions have significant intergenerational effects. Among its several advantages is the fact that our proposed approach is based on individuals' *own*
valuations of future benefits and costs, as well as their *own* views as to
how future effects ought to be traded off against present ones. In that
sense, the mock referendum approach would seem to fit more comfort-
ably within the traditional conception of a welfare economics anchored
squarely in individual preferences.

In the following section, we discuss the difficulties that the DFD
approach confronts when applied to problems like global climate change,

difficulties related both to valuation and to discounting. Next, we present our proposed alternative, the mock referendum, and discuss its advantages and, importantly, the primary disadvantage it raises. There we point out that, in addition to its philosophical and analytical appeal, the mock referendum is also attractive for a very practical reason: it mimics the political determination that must be made—either directly by voters, or by their elected representatives—if climate mitigation measures are ever to be taken. We conclude with a statement of our interest in an ambitious and potentially important application of our proposed approach.

SHORTCOMINGS OF THE DFD APPROACH

Anyone familiar with benefit-cost analysis—and certainly anyone who has contemplated its application to an issue like global climate change—is aware of the problems posed by the DFD approach. First, and obviously, it requires one to estimate in dollar terms the benefits and costs that will occur in future years. This itself presents several problems. One could conceive of this task as filling in the cells of a matrix in which the columns represent types of benefits and costs. For instance, one column would represent, in dollar terms, the premature mortality that would be forestalled by climate mitigation measures; another column, the real property protected by preventing sea-level rise and more frequent storms; still another, the increased agricultural output a more moderate climate would permit; and so on. Other columns in the matrix, of course, would represent higher fuel prices, lost job opportunities, the inconvenience associated with smaller cars, and any other costs (including some environmental harms) associated with climate mitigation measures. It should go without saying how difficult it can be even to assign dollar values to some benefits and costs that will occur in the immediate future.

The rows in this "effects matrix" would be the years in which the benefits and costs would occur. Thus, obviously, there would be as many rows as there would be years—quite a matrix to contemplate in the case of a nuclear waste disposal program, for instance. How, in this latter case, for instance, would we determine how many fewer cancer cases there might be one hundred years from now (not to mention one thousand or ten thousand years) if nuclear waste disposal methods are made more stringent, when we can have very little idea of what life will be like at that time (just as our forebears in 1896 could scarcely imagine what life would be like today)? What value should we attach to these lives prolonged even if we could confidently enumerate them?

A final complication for this picture is that the values to be attached to each cell in this matrix—say, preventing three hundred deaths in Sri

Lanka in the year 2120—will vary among those individuals alive today. Thus, we really ought to have a three-dimensional matrix in effects (negative and positive), time, and individuals. The latter problem is generally surmounted by assigning "average" values to various types of effects, but we all know that this practice, while providing tractability, is not very satisfactory.

Even if we were comfortable with the values to be attached to different types of benefits and costs at different points in time, we would still need to face the selection of "the" discount rate to use in calculating present values. Chapter 4 of the Working Group III Report (in IPCC 1996) presents two different approaches to selecting the discount rate. The first approach, which the authors of that chapter dub the "prescriptive approach," is, as they put it, "...constructed from ethical principles" (p. 131). The second, or "descriptive approach" involves identification of the rate of return to (or opportunity cost of) capital, appropriately adjusted for risk. According to Chapter 4 of the IPCC report, the former approach generally results in a discount rate in the range of 0.5 to 3.0%, while the latter produces a higher rate, generally in excess of 5% in real terms.

There are problems with either approach. First, the prescriptive approach is premised on the view that there is an ethically or morally "correct" rate of discount to use in project evaluation—a rate that is independent of the views of the present generation (save, of course, those who get to determine what the morally just rate is). Yet those of us who teach benefit-cost analysis and advocate its use in public policymaking generally point approvingly to its democratic nature. That is, we argue that BCA is attractive because it is based on the preferences of all those around today.[2] It ought to make us uncomfortable to assert that the discount rate to be used in the DFD approach can be determined independently of the preferences of those whose values we insist be the basis of the benefit and cost estimates.

Implicit in the search for a descriptive discount rate is the view that a single rate can be found that is appropriate for all situations, and that this rate is constant exponentially. Generally, under the descriptive approach, this is the risk-free rate of return to invested capital. Yet discount rates surely vary among individuals, as illustrated by research using both revealed and stated preference methods (see, for example, Cropper, Aydede, and Portney 1994; Hausman 1979; and Thaler 1981).

Ideally, then, one would like an approach to project valuation that takes account of these differences. In fact, it seems likely that the same individual might discount different types of benefits and costs differently. For instance, Cropper, Aydede, and Portney found that individuals responding to questions about the timing of hypothetical lifesaving programs revealed relatively high discount rates for lives saved even five years into the future—the median rate among 475 individuals was 16.8%, with some individuals revealing much higher rates than this. Although these revealed discount rates for lives saved were similar to the same respondents' revealed discount rates for money, there is no reason to believe that respondents would have traded off future ecosystems preserved, miles of shoreline protected, or other possible benefits or costs for present ones at the same rate(s). Finally, the aforementioned researchers, as well as others, have found evidence suggesting that individuals do not use a constant exponential rate to discount future gains or losses. Generally, the longer the period of time over which the discounting takes place, the lower the discount rate that people apply.

For all these reasons, then, the DFD approach blurs differences between individuals' valuations of environmental benefits and costs, as well as between the rate(s) at which they would trade off their own well-being and that of their fellow travelers in the present period for that of generations yet unborn. Therefore, the DFD approach to some extent flies in the face of individual choice—the bedrock of modern applied welfare economics. Because these shortcomings are so familiar to us all, we sometimes lose sight of how formidable they are. We turn now to an alternative conception of benefit-cost analysis for intergenerational decisionmaking that avoids these difficulties.

THE MOCK REFERENDUM APPROACH

The alternative we propose—the mock referendum—is more tractable than the DFD approach to the analysis of projects with significant intergenerational effects. It is theoretically consistent with notions of preference-based valuation of benefit and cost streams, and also with preference-based discounting of these same streams.

What we have in mind is the following. First, a specific policy proposal is selected for analysis. If global climate change is the problem at issue, the policy might be a tax set at $50 per ton of carbon equivalent, a commitment to stabilize U.S. carbon dioxide (CO_2) emissions at 1990 levels by the year 2010 using marketable permits, or perhaps a commitment by the United States to do its part (however that might be determined) to assure the stabilization of atmospheric concentrations of CO_2 at some level by the year 2050, using a variety of policy instruments. Whatever the case, note that conventional BCA could be conducted using the DFD approach to evaluate any or all of these proposed policies.

Under the mock referendum approach, however, appeal is made directly to the citizenry for the evaluation of the policy option in question. First, a representative random sample of U.S. households is drawn, a sample that could be partitioned in any number of ways (to be discussed below). This sample would then be presented with a detailed description of what is known about the likely effects of the policy change, and—importantly—what is likely to happen if nothing is done. Among other things, that description would spell out the beneficial effects expected to result from the intervention, and where and when they will occur. Examples might include (but not be limited to) lower global average temperatures, implying less incidence of microbially induced premature mortality and morbidity, a reduced likelihood of sea-level rise and associated shoreline losses and saltwater intrusion into freshwater systems, and less disruption of agricultural and silvicultural activities.

It is important that the sample households be presented with the best information possible about where these effects will be felt. For instance, they should be told that a program that prevents, say, a half-meter increase in sea-level rise will do the most good in low-lying undeveloped countries such as Bangladesh (if, in fact, that is what the best science indicates). They might be told that a policy that helps slow forest secession would be especially valuable to some countries or parts of countries, but not to others. And, they might be told that the reduced incidence of vector-borne diseases will do the greatest good in tropical countries where these diseases would be most likely to proliferate.

The descriptive material presented to the sample population would also include a description of how the proposed policy intervention would work. That is, it would explain how a tax on carbon equivalents, say, would translate into increased prices for gasoline, home heating oil, electricity, and other products not initially subject to the tax but making use of the taxed products as inputs. Again, it is very important in this description to indicate the spatial distribution of these costs, *including the consequences likely to be borne by the households being surveyed.* In other words, those living in the Midwest who are served by electric utility systems heavily dependent on coal would be told that increased electricity prices in their region are likely to be higher than those in, say, the Pacific Northwest, and by how much. They would also need to be made aware that policies that have their initial cost impacts felt in the United States could, nevertheless, affect foreign countries. This could happen, for example, through a reduction in imports from developing countries if tax increases in the United States slowed economic growth. Other expected cost impacts would have to be described, as well.

It is quite important that the temporal distribution of impacts be described as carefully as possible. Households would need to be told what favorable and unfavorable impacts are likely to occur immediately, which ones could be expected later in their lives (say, over the next twenty to thirty years), and which impacts are not likely to manifest themselves for hundreds of years. It is equally important that households be given a sense of the uncertainties that attach to the various effects. For instance, they might be told, "Scientists are relatively certain that, in the absence of a reduction in greenhouse gas emissions, any significant increase in sea level is unlikely to occur in the next fifty years. However, effects on agriculture could become evident in this time." They might also be told, to illustrate this point, "While the most likely effect of this policy on energy prices is an $X\%$ increase, there are many who believe that energy conservation and the accelerated adoption of renewable energy sources will make it possible to meet the goals of this policy with much less sacrifice. In fact, there are some experts (a minority) who believe that these policies may end up costing little or nothing."

The material in foregoing quotes above would represent a small part of the descriptive material that would be presented to the households being surveyed. Needless to say, great care would need to be taken in preparing this descriptive material, in the same way many cities and states take care in the preparation of the materials available to voters in advance of referenda items on state and local ballots. To reiterate, the materials would need to provide the most balanced information possible about the likely benefits and costs, across both space and time, associated with the proposed policy change. This information should also include a description of what other countries will be doing to address the problems associated with climate change. For instance, the materials might indicate that, "In addition to these measures being contemplated in the United States, other countries including Germany, Japan, Great Britain, France, and… will also be taking similar actions." To get ahead of ourselves a bit here, the descriptive materials that households receive could be varied on this point. For instance, some households might receive materials indicating that, "While the United States is moving ahead to address this possible threat, other countries are still deliberating. It is possible that we will be acting alone for some number of years."

The most important respect in which the descriptive material would vary concerns the description of the costs that the household itself is likely to bear, now and in the future. By confronting households with identical information on the likely beneficial effects of the program in space and time, and identical information on the costs that others are likely to bear, while varying for different respondents the description of the costs that they are likely to face, one can sketch out a willingness-to-pay (WTP) locus for the policy by observing the way their (hypothetical) votes vary with the cost of the program. This is the kernel of our proposed mock referendum approach.

By varying other information provided to subsets of respondents, we can learn how sensitive their votes (or WTP) would be to the seriousness of the adverse effects likely to result from inaction, the uncertainties conveyed in the descriptive material, the timing of the effects, and their spatial distribution. In addition—because one would also collect information about the respondents' attitudes, incomes, education, and other socioeconomic characteristics—it would be possible to estimate a WTP equation. This in turn would enable the prediction of individual responses in a mock or actual referendum based on a knowledge of individuals' characteristics.

The appeal of this approach, we believe, is that individual "voting" reveals four important bits of information with which one would struggle in the DFD approach.

- The vote indicates an up-or-down decision on the policy as described to the household, and in this way provides an implicit estimate of the net benefits of a proposed policy.
- This decision forces the household to aggregate the values it implicitly attaches to the various benefit and cost categories—for example, the reduced risk of premature mortality in equatorial countries, the reduced likelihood of Kansas farmers suffering income losses, and so on.
- The mock referendum approach forces each respondent to discount *at his or her own rate* the benefits and costs that will be felt at different points in time. Thus, for example, a respondent who cares a great deal about those in less developed countries, even those that will inhabit these countries several generations hence, will be more likely to vote yes than one who cares less about what will happen farther away in time and space. In other words, our proposed approach recognizes the heterogeneity of individual preferences on discount rates, rather than forces the artificial selection of a single rate to use.
- Depending on the ambitiousness of the sample size, one can capture all the heterogeneity that exists across households and thus be sure that the results approximate what might happen if such an issue were put to a vote.

For all these reasons, then, we think the mock referendum approach is more attractive on intellectual grounds than the DFD approach *for these types of problems*.

Note also that our proposed approach is in one sense quite consistent with the "options" view of decisionmaking under great uncertainty. (See, for example, the paper by Robert Lind in Chapter 17 of this volume.) That is, referenda like the one we propose here could be conducted every so often. This would enable one to reflect in the descriptive material provided to respondents any new knowledge or developments relevant to the likely benefits and costs associated with possible policy interventions.

Thus, for instance, if fuel cells become economically competitive with traditional fossil fuels at a faster rate than is currently anticipated, a mock referendum in ten years would present to respondents more favorable information on the expected costs of the policy. Similarly, if new research in atmospheric chemistry suddenly began to undercut the case for mitigation measures, that, too, could be reflected in the materials provided to respondents in mock referenda. Over time, then, the accretion of new science would influence respondents' votes; it might strengthen the case for certain kinds of protective "hedges," while also shedding light on the value of options purchased in the past.

There is another reason why the mock referendum approach appeals to us for the analysis of problems with significant intergenerational consequences: it provides the information that must be known if the United States, or any other democracy for that matter, is to take significant actions to reduce emissions of greenhouse gases, begin the construction of radioactive waste repositories, or engage in significant preservation of the habitat of endangered species. To put the matter bluntly, it makes little difference what a benefit-cost analysis premised on the DFD approach says if the American public thinks it silly to spend its money on a program with very speculative benefits that, even should they occur, will go to those in faraway countries hundreds of years hence. Not only does the mock referendum approach provide information on implicit values and rates of time preference, but it also gives us a foreshadowing of what our elected representatives will need to know if and when the time comes to vote on a climate control or other type of program.

PROBLEMS WITH THE MOCK REFERENDUM

We are not so naive as to be blind to the shortcomings of the approach we put forward here. It goes without saying that these are the shortcomings associated with the contingent valuation method. Can we provide respondents with a manageable amount of information sufficient to allow them to cast a minimally informed "vote"? What confidence can we have that their hypothetical votes are at all indicative of what would happen if the decision were really left to them in a national plebiscite? And so on.

We will say little here about this latter question, other than to note that Senator Robert Dole was given virtually no chance by anyone of winning the 1996 presidential election because opinion polls taken at various times prior to that election indicated that he had very little support. These polls, which were borne out on Election Day, were of course based on respondents' *stated* intentions. We should also note that the DFD approach to benefit-cost analysis does not avoid the problems associated with the absence of revealed preferences. Other than through the use of stated preference approaches, how will the benefits of species preservation—to take but one example—be valued for traditional application of the DFD approach?

We would like to address the former difficulty associated with our proposed approach—namely, how informed could respondents be in our mock referendum if all they are given is several pages of materials describing what might happen in both the presence and the absence of a policy change designed to deal with, say, global climate change? This is problematical, of course, especially given the very great uncertainties that attend estimates of physical effects, their associated socioeconomic impacts, the costs of mitigation and adaptation, the time and spatial distribution of effects, and so on. We are under no illusion here that we can provide respondents with the information available, say, to the experts participating in the IPCC (though they tend to be specialized in their expertise), or even to policymakers in governments contemplating climate mitigation measures.

We do, however, believe it is possible to provide respondents with perhaps as much clear and objective information as would be available to many members of the Senate who would be required to vote on the 1997 Kyoto protocol if that treaty is ever submitted for ratification. We may be wrong, but it is our conjecture that congressional voting would be relatively uninformed if a measure like one of those described earlier were brought before our elected representatives. The materials they would be likely to have seen would come from partisans on both sides of the debate; the hearings they may have attended (though this is unlikely) would have featured these same partisans, and perhaps an occasional middle-of-the-roader with five minutes to make his or her point; and the visits they would have been paid would likewise have been from these advocates. We think we can provide sufficient information to allow "voters" to make an intelligent choice in a mock referendum. Will this information be oversimplified? Of course, but no more oversimplified than the information members of the U.S. Congress will have if and when they are asked to decide on this question.

FINAL THOUGHTS

We would be upset if this paper were construed as a rejection of the DFD approach for all environmental policy analysis. To the contrary, we strongly support its use in most environmental decisions, and believe that it can highlight important trade-offs and make them transparent to all affected parties. Indeed, it would seem to be a necessary condition for good decisionmaking and we support its widespread application.

However, the class of problem discussed here—those for which many of the important benefits and costs will not arise for hundreds of years or more—may tax traditional BCA beyond its limits. It requires us to make estimates of changes in physical effects (such as lives saved, ecosystems preserved, miles of shoreline protected) so far away in time as to be essentially meaningless. It also requires us to come up with values for every one of these effects when, we must admit, we can have no very good idea of what our distant descendants will and will not value. Of greater relevance to the subject of this workshop, the DFD approach then requires us to select one discount rate to use to telescope these distant benefits and costs back to the present when, in fact, we recognize that each individual trades off future for present well-being (and even different attributes of well-being) at a different rate.

While hardly a panacea, the alternative we propose—a mock referendum—gets around these problems in a way we find attractive. It places the burden of valuation and discounting for intergenerational projects squarely on the shoulders of those who would begin to bear the burdens associated with project implementation—those in the here and now. If repeated regularly, it could be updated as old generations die off and are replaced by new ones. In that regard, it is more consistent with the individualistic underpinnings of applied welfare economics than is the DFD approach. In addition, it mimics the political reality concerning projects with significant intergenerational effects. If the voting public does not regard the uncertain benefits of these projects (benefits that are at least partially remote in both space and time) as being worth the costs that must be borne now, they will not support their adoption, purely and simply.

Why not include in the analytical arsenal a tool that sheds light on valuation, discounting, and political acceptability all at the same time? We think a study making use of the mock referendum would be a useful addition to existing analyses of climate mitigation policies, and we would be willing to discuss the design and conduct of such a study with any and all interested parties.

ENDNOTES

[1]This abstracts from the so-called ancillary benefits that may be associated with carbon mitigation strategies—for example, reductions in ambient concentrations of particulate matter and photochemical oxidants—that could be felt immediately. These should be given increased attention in analyses of proposed climate policies.

[2]To be sure, we sometimes also lament the preferences of our contemporaries, such as when they give rise to the salary differentials that exist between, say, Madonna on the one hand and the country's best high school mathematics teacher on the other. We must also acknowledge that the preferences of the rich receive more weight in BCA than those of the poor because they are backed by more dollar "votes." Finally, we must acknowledge that we can only guess in BCA at the values that future generations would attach to various kinds of benefits and costs.

REFERENCES

Cropper, Maureen L., Sema K. Aydede, and Paul R. Portney. 1994. Preferences for Life Saving Programs: How the Public Discounts Time and Age. *Journal of Risk and Uncertainty* 8: 243–66.

Hausman, Jerry A. 1979. Individual Discount Rates and the Purchase and Utilization of Energy Using Durables. *The Bell Journal of Economics* 10: 33–54.

IPCC (Intergovernmental Panel on Climate Change). 1996. *Climate Change 1995: Economic and Social Dimensions of Climate Change*. Contribution of Working Group III to the Second Assessment Report of the IPCC. New York: Cambridge University Press.

Kneese, Allen V. 1973. The Faustian Bargain. *Resources* 44: 1–5. Reprinted in Wallace E. Oates (ed.). 1999. *The RFF Reader in Environmental and Resource Management*. Washington, D.C.: Resources for the Future.

Thaler, Richard. 1981. Some Empirical Evidence on Dynamic Inconsistency. *Economic Letters* 8: 201–07.

10

Intergenerational Discounting

Thomas C. Schelling

My interest is the special case of discounting *benefits* of greenhouse gas abatement. Discounting *costs* poses no new problem; costs for most of the first fifty years will be borne by governments or publics in the already developed countries. Most of the benefits will accrue in the second fifty years from now, and will accrue to the descendants of people in the now-developing countries. We can expect most of those beneficiaries to be much better off than their current ancestors, but probably not yet as well off as the people in the currently developed countries are now. Any abatement program is essentially a foreign aid program.

Any damages due to climate change will be slow in coming. Greenhouse gas concentrations (probably in contrast to emissions) will continue to increase throughout the coming century, so that differences in climate during the first fifty years will be significantly less than differences from present climates that will be registered in the second fifty years.

There are three reasons why the beneficiaries will mainly be the descendants of people in the currently poorer countries. First, that is where the people are, four-fifths of them now, and nine-tenths in the second fifty years. Second, it is the developing countries whose economies are currently susceptible to climate, and in fifty years will probably still be more susceptible to climate than the economies of the now-developed countries. And third, while most of the developing countries may enjoy more rapid economic growth over the next fifty years than the currently developed economies, in that second half century from now they will almost certainly be at lower levels of per capita income than their contemporaries in the developed countries. As far as material welfare is con-

THOMAS C. SCHELLING is a professor of economics and public affairs at the University of Maryland and the Lucius N. Littauer Professor of Political Economy, Emeritus, at Harvard University.

cerned, therefore, by almost any plausible measure, the benefits will be distributed as I have described.

Any model that treats greenhouse gas abatement as a matter of investing now in order to reap future benefits, as in domestic environmental programs, is simply inappropriate. There can be, for example, no "time preference" of the traditional sort. Time preference, often associated with impatience, relates to impatience about one's own future consumption, that is, the consumption in the future by the person who currently forgoes consumption in the interest of investment. Greenhouse gas abatement is a foreign aid program, not a saving-investment program of the familiar kind. One can be more interested in the welfare of Chinese and Indian children born in 2050 than in those born in 2075, or in 2100, but that would hardly be due to impatience or any of the usual ingredients of time preference.

Another component usually embedded in intergenerational discounting is the trajectory of the marginal utility of consumption of the beneficiaries. It is often expressed as some (constant) elasticity of marginal utility with respect to the level of consumption, multiplied by some anticipated rate of growth in the level of consumption. Since the level of consumption is increasing, and has been increasing for several decades, in almost all parts of the world, this marginal-utility component of a discount rate is assumed positive.

But the fact that the level of consumption is likely to be increasing in most of the world does not mean that the beneficiaries of greenhouse gas abatement will have higher levels of consumption than the people who invest in that greenhouse gas abatement. We in North America, Western Europe, and Japan will be investing in greenhouse gas abatement for the benefit of people who in fifty or seventy-five years will probably still be poorer than we are now.

If instead we all invested for the benefit of our own descendants, so that Americans were investing in the welfare of their great grandchildren and the Chinese were doing the same, the projected rise in per capita consumption and associated lower marginal utility of consumption would indeed provide an argument for a positive component in a discount rate. Still, it seems unlikely to me that in thinking about transferring welfare to their substantially more wealthy descendants we could reasonably expect today's citizens in China (or, for that matter, in the United States) to acquiesce in transfers (from poor to rich) simply because the increment in consumption, compared with the current decrement, is large enough to offset the diminished marginal utility.

We have little practice in thinking about deliberate transfers from the less well-to-do to the more well-to-do. Arthur Okun used to talk about the "leaky bucket" in which we necessarily transferred income from the wealthy to the poor; there were administrative costs and deadweight losses and some target inefficiencies in making the transfers. He never had to worry about a bucket in which the good things multiplied in transit so that more arrived at the destination than was removed from the origin, and the criterion might be whether the growth of good things in transit outweighed the lesser marginal utility of the wealthy beneficiaries.

But we don't have to worry about it either because with greenhouse gas abatement, in contrast to things like domestic pesticide abatement or toxic waste abatement, the transfers would be from the people who will be living in the coming decades in western Europe, North America, and Japan, to people living elsewhere in the decades after that.

The real significance of the diminishing marginal utility of consumption, that is, of discounting future increments to consumption, is in the choice between helping, with material assistance, the early generations in the developing countries or the later generations. Most of the populations in today's developing countries range from quite poor to desperately poor. Their descendants in the second half of the coming century—the beneficiaries of greenhouse gas abatement—we expect to be much less poor. There is no way that we can accelerate the benefits of greenhouse gas abatement in order to enhance living standards during the next few decades. If the people in western Europe, North America, and Japan are to be persuaded to sacrifice some material welfare in the coming decades for beneficiaries in the rest of the world, there is a choice between investing in immediate economic improvement in those countries or investing in improvement that will begin to be felt fifty years from now.

Investing in immediate improvement has two things to say for it. One is that raising material welfare now—not just consumption, but health and safety—meets a more urgent need. The second is that economic development may be the best defense against any possible adverse effects of climate change. We must always consider, when investing in greenhouse gas abatement for the benefit of those future people, the opportunity cost of investing now in more rapid development for the benefit not only of those future people but of their equally worthy and more needy ancestors.

I see little evidence, at least in the United States, that people want to make significant additional sacrifices to raise living standards among the people who live now in the developing world. It would surprise me if they could get excited about raising living standards in those same parts of the world at a time in the future when those living standards will be, we may both hope and expect, substantially elevated over where they are now.

11

Intergenerational Ethics, Efficiency, and Commitment

Comments on Schelling and Kopp and Portney

Jerome Rothenberg

SCHELLING: INTERGENERATIONAL DISCOUNTING

I strongly agree with Thomas Schelling's central tenet: in decisions about policies concerning global warming, an abatement program initiated by members of the present generation will involve their paying the costs of the program but receiving none or nearly none of the benefits during their lifetime. The benefits for what they do will go to the members of future generations. Evaluating such a program in the present, therefore, requires comparing costs to one generation with benefits to other generations. So, the standard paradigm of intertemporal resource allocation does not apply, where resource uses are shifted across the lifetime of a single generation to maximize the present discounted value of *that generation's lifetime consumption*.

Continuous time discounting, via private sector or social discount rates, has optimality properties in such a paradigm but not where intergenerational comparisons are involved. For one thing, there is no place for pure time preference in the usual sense of impatience: events occurring at different times beyond the lifetime of the present generation are irrelevant to the actual experiences of this generation. The significance of events happening to future generations depends on either a normative principle or some perceptual/emotional feelings aroused by contemplating such diverse futures "today."

JEROME ROTHENBERG is Professor Emeritus of Economics at the Massachusetts Institute of Technology.

I do not believe any generation abides by a general normative principle widely and strongly enough to determine its actual intertemporal behavior. So, I lean on a behavioristic interpretation of a social discount rate: the weight felt to be appropriate to members of any particular future generation depends on how well off they are expected to be (and how that living standard translates into personal utility per unit of monetary gain or loss), and how much empathy that generation arouses in the present generation.

Prediction of an upward trend in per capita income would introduce a continuous positive time discount factor in its evaluation. But the second factor operates differently. Differential weights refer to specific generations: they reflect differential degrees of "empathic distance" from the present generation, a concept used by Schelling as well. "Empathic distance" is the closeness of emotional and imaginative linkages with the present generation. Nearly undisturbed genetic makeups—that is, close lineal descendants—and cultural, norm, value, and living-pattern similarities determine relative nearness. By this measure, distance in future is associated with weakening linkages. But, perceptual differences between generations decrease with greater remoteness, until a point at which all future generations have the same nearly anonymous fuzziness.

This second component, "generation discount weights," therefore, has the following form: each future generation is given the same weight *over its entire lifetime*, and the immediate next generation has a high weight because of direct biological descendance, followed by a significant discrete decline to the next generation; with smaller subsequent discrete declines for a few more generations, then all further generations receive the same nonzero weight. The result overall, then, is a declining step function that remains significantly greater than zero into the indefinite future. The combination of the two components will be a declining function, continuous with future generations, but subject to discrete declines at generation boundaries. Whether the well-being or empathic component dominates depends on expectations about future well-being. Extreme optimism or pessimism will make this factor dominate. Mainstream economists may, however, be currently more optimistic than the public generally, who seem more uncertain about the future. If so, then the structure of altruism given by empathic distance will dominate the social discount rate, and far future generations will be accorded nontrivial evaluational weights.

Schelling wants to use the benefit-cost separation between present and future generations, along with the absence of true time preference, to treat climate-change abatement policy as simply a matter of income redistributions. For this purpose, he disaggregates the population of each generation. His analysis of how abatement programs are likely to work leads him to conclude that the richest portion of the present generation will be largely subsidizing the poorest portion of far future generations. So, the program represents a progressive income redistribution. But, its overall attractiveness must be compared with other possible income redistributions open to the present generation—which represent for Schelling the same ethical issue. Since Schelling predicts a substantial upward trend in global per capita income, the poorest in the remote future will be considerably richer than the poorest in the present generation. Foreign aid for the present generation, therefore, represents a more productive redistribution than the redistribution attached to abatement.

Schelling oversimplifies in translating the global climate abatement issue solely as one of income redistribution. The benefit-cost generational split is not sufficient to eliminate intertemporal efficiency from the problem. Indeed, I believe that efficiency is the heart of the problem. The issue is intergenerational externalities.

In an overlapping generations model with complete property rights over all assets, assets owned by the present generation with durability or productivity that can affect the future generations have a value that can be turned into late consumption or increased value of bequests to descendants by the present generation's selling them to representatives of the next generation. So, all decisions by the present generation that affect such assets (amount, quality, and so forth) also affect their exchange values, and so, this generation has an incentive to balance immediate gains from their creation and use with future gains near the end of their lifetimes. This presumably leads to efficient intertemporal—but intragenerational—resource allocation.

Now, if property rights are incomplete, as with the status of the climatic system—environmental capital—Generation 1 cannot sell such assets to the future. Decreases in its quality from present resource uses then do not decrease Generation 1's welfare, since that quality has no market value to it—though it certainly has a welfare value to Generation 2 and beyond. The result is that Generation 1 has no direct incentive to structure its activities to balance damages to future generations via greenhouse gas emissions (in each activity, such damages are given no weight as a cost) against gains to itself via the consumption-estate consequences of those activities. Thus, negative intergenerational externalities are generated via emissions that are not included in the efficiency calculus. So long as those damages mean anything to Generation 1, it is behaving inefficiently. "Abatement" programs are simply a generic name for a family of efforts to correct real prices facing Generation 1 via charges, regulations, technological fixes, and so forth.

This viewpoint, incidentally, determines, in principle, how much, if any, "abatement" should be carried out—something that Schelling's approach avows to be inconclusive, a matter of political decision alone. Here, it is a familiar balancing of the present value of marginal future damages avoided with marginal present abatement costs.

The present decision situation has two parts: Is any form of abatement warranted now? What form of abatement is best? For the latter, we have two main classes: prevention and adaptation. The first of these is the familiar family of present "corrections." The latter is important because of the long gestation period of future damages and of the effects of corrections. It consists in measures and/or assets (including new technology) designed to increase the ability of future generations to adapt to the changing climate as it happens and, thereby, to decrease the damages that occur. A subset of these is to make provision for a general subsidizing of those generations in terms of overall productivity—in effect, a reimbursement to them for sustaining unmitigated climatic damages.

All forms of abatement represent investments on behalf of the future. As such, they must be funded in the present. That means they must be committed through several future generations to reach the remote generations for whom damages are greatest. Prevention measures represent a somewhat more tangible physical commitment than adaptation and reimbursement because of their durability and the adjustment costs involved in a future attempt at undoing. If strong commitment to avoid interim undoing can nonetheless be achieved for adaptation/reimbursement, then the productivity of these investments—variously approximated by market rates of return on capital—becomes the opportunity cost of preventive abatement relative to these.

But, the problem of intergenerational commitment is a difficult one. Future evaluations, needs, and preferences may well change and result in measures that violate the intentions of Generation 1. Space will not permit discussion of these beyond the following brief notes.

- No one generational abatement effort can have more than a trivial effect on the future. Not only must future generations not dilute or distort present actions, they must continue the same basic strategy with their own abatement.
- Different types of present abatement have different likelihoods of being continued. As suggested earlier, efforts involving specialized durable capital impose greater commitment because their undoing is costly; those involving simply investing in higher overall future productivity are easier to tamper with.
- The propensity of future generations to "spoil" an abatement effort must not be overstated. If Generation 1 acts on a clear policy principle, abetted by operationally transparent decision procedures, it becomes easy for future generations to follow it with continuity. If

they do not, it may be because of new information, or new technology. Generation 1, faced with such updating, would presumably have modified its own actions accordingly. A change in tastes regarding present versus future is a different story. But, there is no normative principle that argues that the earlier values have greater normative weight and should prevail over later values.

Suppose adaptational/reimbursement actions are not explicitly "funded" (earmarked, dedicated). It is sometimes argued that even here the opportunity cost of abatement generally is the rate of return on private capital. This presumes that abatement costs come only at the expense of private investment. This is not so. Such costs decrease both investment and consumption. So, the social discount rate must be used, not the return on private investment.

Finally, a general argument against my approach is that it is unfair to single out the *negative* externalities imposed by the present generation on the future; its actions, in general, benefit the future; hence, the upward trend in per capita income over time. The negative externalities are simply a necessary cost to achieve such overall advances. This argument assumes that every negative externality is directly attached to actions that generate future improvement. This is not so. Emissions result from activities that generally affect the present generation more than the future. The efficiency argument is that *certain* present activities, and only in *certain ways* of carrying them out, generate these diseconomies. These activities, and these ways, are not dependably generated by positive effects on the future. To correct the incentives toward the former resource uses does not automatically hurt the future.

KOPP AND PORTNEY: MOCK REFERENDA FOR INTERGENERATIONAL DECISIONMAKING

I strongly agree with the assertion by Ray Kopp and Paul Portney that the use of the standard damage function and discounting approach to benefit-cost analysis is deeply flawed when applied to extremely long-duration projects like greenhouse gas abatement. Their suggested mock referendum technique is advanced to bypass these flaws. I hold mixed views, though, on how well it can do so.

The procedure is a form of contingent valuation technique. It is favored because it permits the public itself to express its preferences about them in the policy decision. Also, it will permit different individuals to use the different personal discounting rates that the authors are convinced empirically obtain in the population, instead of imposing a single discount rate from outside.

The mock referendum approach seeks explicit valuation from its respondents for all of the kinds of effects (benefit and cost), to whom, and when. It selects random samples that are expected to reflect real-world differences in tastes, perspectives, socioeconomic circumstances, perspectives, knowledge, and "special interests." Each respondent is expected to give component valuations, to discount these valuations, and to aggregate across the different types of discounted effects. The procedure then aggregates across the sample respondents to give a "social value" of benefits and costs.

The method is, of course, subject to all the usual difficulties associated with contingent valuation. In the present application, it has an additional critical problem: the informedness of the respondents. The question is, how credible is the degree of their informedness and how stable are the resulting valuations? "Informedness" is not simply what information is explicitly given to the respondents as part of the survey. It concerns more deeply whether their *experience* of the positive and negative effects involved is deep enough to elicit coherent judgments.

The strength of market behavior in revealing preference is due to the fact that the commodities involved are those actually consumed by the market participants: these are personal, not simply private, goods. Where the goods have aspects of publicness, along with private consumption, individual valuation is less trustworthy because perceived worth depends partly on the hypothetical or expected behavior of others with respect to the good (for example, expected density in use of roads, beach, park, museum). Where the good is entirely public, with no personal consumption, the perception is even less well defined. In the present case, there is no personal consumption involved, only circumstances for other people—and these circumstances can refer to complex aspects of a way of life—and this way of life can be extremely vague to the respondents because they refer to people in the far future whose overall circumstances and habits and values and tastes may be utterly inaccessible to the respondents. This is a situation where remoteness in time refers as much to *visualizing* how the policy consequences will affect real, but different, people as it does to the *importance* of the people in those remote generations to present respondents.

Also related to remoteness is the high degree of uncertainty about every aspect of the problem—both the possible unmitigated climate changes and their complex multifaceted effects on people, and the possible effects of the program in question on both. People are notably shaky about even simple joint probability distributions, let alone those relating to the effects on the structure and stability of societies with possible massive reallocations of activity and population migrations. Moreover, the effects are significantly interrelated, rather than linearly independent.

Descriptions of lists of effects will not convey the *significance* of complexes of these effects. This last point is associated with the ability of respondents to aggregate *across* different types of effects. More than summation is surely required.

A further problem is that program effects are similarly not linear. Their effectiveness depends on scale, in this kind of program on international scale. The worthwhileness of a *national* program, given the world commons scale of the phenomenon, depends on which and how many other countries are or will be conditionally linked to this (with all of the uncertainty associated with this) program. Information of this sort must be part of what is conveyed to respondents.

Given these obstacles to tolerable respondent "informedness," "raw" surveys are not likely to elicit credible responses. My approach to this problem is to use an intervening stage in the procedure. I would use a panel of technical experts to "interpret" different possible sets of outcomes by means of "scores" or indexes—thereby carrying out a form of partial aggregation converting masses of often highly interrelated kinds of effects into judgments about "how serious" are the disruptions of "normal life." It is these index levels of outcomes that are conveyed to the respondents; they must then indicate how important such comparisons are to them.

The Kopp and Portney mock referendum may be a very important research technique for helping to clarify the complexities of valuation in these applications. Because of the numerous difficulties involved, the technique can be used *experimentally* to reveal the sensitivity of respondent valuations to different aspects of the information conveyed—for example, what is due to the complexities of social system interrelatedness. Elements in this survey would be experimentally varied to elicit such revelations. Staggered repetitions would seek to discover the stability of responses. Different respondent samples would be taken to examine the effects of population heterogeneity. In all of these, the distribution of replies would be carefully monitored.

The mock referendum technique has high potential to teach us a great deal about how real people handle valuation in areas as problematic as this. What we learn cannot help but furnish us with ideas about how to improve actual social variations in these areas.

12

Equity, Efficiency, and Discounting

Alan S. Manne

There are descriptive and there are prescriptive views on time discounting. A "descriptive" benchmark is provided by market rates of discount. "Prescriptive" views are closely related to the ideas of equity and fairness. Equity and efficiency may be separated when greenhouse policies are to be implemented within a decentralized market framework, and no major changes are proposed in the ownership of labor, capital, and other conventional resources. A commonsense way to describe equity-efficiency separability conditions is that global climate change will be limited sufficiently so that most prices and discount rates will not change much.

Several of these ideas are illustrated through a small-scale numerical model contrasting the ILA (infinite-lived agent) versus the OLG (overlapping generations) perspectives. ILA and OLG represent two polar-opposite viewpoints on intergenerational altruism, but they need not differ in their implications for economically efficient agreements on greenhouse gas abatement.

WHERE (ALMOST) EVERYONE AGREES

Future generations are likely to be wealthier in terms of labor productivity and in conventional forms of capital. They will probably be poorer in terms of environmental resources. In relation to conventional goods and services, the value of environmental resources is therefore likely to rise over time. Hereafter, in referring to "the" discount rate, we will mean the discount rate on conventional goods and services.

ALAN S. MANNE is an emeritus professor, Department of Engineering—Economic Systems and Operations Research, Stanford University.

The greenhouse gas problem is global in scale. It represents a "public good" problem. If we need to proceed beyond "no regrets" policies, there will have to be international agreements for abatement and for burden-sharing between regions and over time.

International negotiations have focused on carbon dioxide. Annual emissions are small in relation to the existing stock of atmospheric carbon. This means that abatement costs are borne early, and benefits do not accrue until the distant future. That is why the discount rate plays a crucial role in the greenhouse debate.

Both the costs and the benefits of abatement are uncertain. The lower the discount rate, the greater becomes the sensitivity of near-future decisions to distant-future parameters that are inherently uncertain. With uncertainty, it is sensible to adopt a hedging strategy based on sequential decision making. As a guide to decisions during the next few decades, it is more important to agree upon the discount rate during these decades rather than during the very distant future.

WHERE THERE IS DISAGREEMENT

As is well known, there are descriptive and there are prescriptive views on time discounting. Rather than review the literature here, the reader is referred to Chapter 4 of IPPC 1996.

A "descriptive" benchmark is provided by market rates of discount. Along a time path that is economically efficient, the market rate will equal the marginal productivity of capital and also the rate of discount on consumption goods. For efficient abatement policies, one would discount both the costs and the benefits at these rates. In attempting to design "first best" (or "second best") policies, there is no reason to distinguish between the discount rates employed for evaluating conventional and environmental capital formation. Currently, these rates (before taxes and net of inflation) are 5% per year or more. For empirical evidence along these lines, see Nordhaus (1994, 125–29).

"Prescriptive" views are closely related to the ideas of equity and fairness. If positive abatement costs are to be incurred, how should the costs be shared among different nations and different generations? What might be an equitable arrangement for cost sharing? Might market rates of discount lead to emission paths that are unsustainable over the long term? Despite the difficulties in international negotiations, it is instructive to consider cooperative decisions in which individual nations/regions strive for Pareto-optimality, and do not engage in threats and gaming. An economically efficient abatement policy requires JI (joint implementation), that is, equalizing the marginal cost of abatement between groups at each point in time.

Why be so concerned about economic efficiency? Under the current rules of the game, an international carbon agreement would have to be reached by unanimous consensus among the participating sovereign nations. At a 5% discount rate, most analyses indicate that the aggregate discounted benefits of an optimal abatement policy would not greatly exceed the benefits of a more gradual move toward long-term sustainability. In order to ensure that there is a potential for each participant to gain from an international agreement, efficiency becomes a necessary precondition.

THE SEPARATION OF EQUITY AND EFFICIENCY ISSUES

Equity and efficiency issues may be separated when greenhouse policies are to be implemented within a decentralized market framework, and no major changes are proposed in the ownership of labor, capital, and other conventional resources. International and intergenerational wealth transfers are designed only to facilitate the sharing of abatement costs—not as a substitute for foreign aid from wealthier to poorer nations, nor as a substitute for transfers from wealthier to poorer generations. For a very different point of view on separability, see Chichilnisky and Heal (1994).

It will not be easy to agree on ways to achieve efficient multilateral JI. Suppose, however, that it were feasible to separate the issue of efficiency from that of equity. The time path of global emissions could then be determined independently of the contentious issue of how to ensure fairness in abatement cost sharing. An international technical organization might recommend the number of carbon emission permits to be distributed on an annual or five-year basis. These permits would in turn be tradeable on an open international market. The worldwide rate of permit sales could be based on principles of intertemporal economic efficiency—that is, through a comparison of discounted costs and benefits.

The equity issues would focus on the allocation of the shares of individual nations in the global total. Some would urge that population be the sole criterion for such shares, and others would point to the importance of existing emissions and the projected growth in these emissions. There would be much of the same type of posturing that takes place within the Organization of Petroleum Exporting Countries for the allocation of oil production quotas.

In global carbon abatement, it is—at least in principle—possible to separate efficiency from equity issues when either of the following is approximately true:

- the benefits of reducing global climate change can be described in terms of the market value of damages avoided; in this case, global climate change affects the economywide production function (such as through coastline erosion or losses in agricultural output); or
- the benefits of reducing global climate change can be described in terms of "willingness-to-pay" to avoid nonmarket damages; in this case, it affects the utility function of individual groups (such as through losses in biodiversity or the hazards of diverting the Gulf Stream).

Presumably, high-income countries would have a greater willingness than poor countries to pay to avoid nonmarket losses. A commonsense way to describe equity-efficiency separability conditions is that global climate change will be limited sufficiently so that most prices and discount rates will not change much. There will not be a significant effect upon the productivity of capital and/or the real incomes (hence the willingness-to-pay) of each group.

THE ILA AND OLG PERSPECTIVES
ON INTERGENERATIONAL ALTRUISM

In order to compare the costs and benefits of alternative abatement strategies, one requires some type of model for the integrated assessment of global climate change. Regardless of whether this model is simple or complex, it has been typical to summarize the results in terms of the ILA paradigm. See, for example, Cline 1992; Peck and Teisberg 1992; Nordhaus 1994; and Manne, Mendelsohn, and Richels 1995. In each of these models, the economy is analyzed as though there were a single agent acting as a trustee on behalf of both the present and future generations. Taken literally, however, ILA is vulnerable to the line of criticism that has been noted by Schelling (1995):

> This assumption of the immortal agent ... supposes that, whoever they are who pay for the investments that lead to increments in future consumption, they value increments in other people's utility as if they were increments in their own utility. It is this willingness to model all humankind as a single agent that makes optimization models attractive, feasible and inappropriate.

Schelling's critique indicates why it might be instructive to compare the ILA with an OLG approach with no bequest motives. ILA and OLG represent two polar-opposite viewpoints on intergenerational altruism, but they need not differ in their implications for economically efficient agreements on greenhouse gas abatement. With OLG, even though each age cohort may operate with no bequest motive and no altruism toward future generations, it does have an incentive to save during its working years and to dissave during retirement. A strictly concave utility function implies that it is optimal to smooth out the life-cycle pattern of consumption. With OLG, there is still an incentive to provide current abatement in order to reduce future damages attributable to climate change. Reducing the growth of greenhouse gas concentrations is a straightforward alternative to physical capital formation. This is not a novel observation. The basic idea has already been suggested by Mäler (1994).

To illustrate these ideas through a highly stylized comparison, it is instructive to construct a small-scale numerical model in which each age cohort has a known and finite life. Each cohort is concerned only with the discounted utility of its personal consumption during that period. There is a perfect market for borrowing, lending, and lifetime annuities, and there is no risk of default.

The world is viewed as though it were a single region operating as a market economy. The model is focused upon economic efficiency within an intergenerational context. It does not address intragenerational distributive issues.

The macro aspects are based upon a standard neoclassical optimal growth model. The labor force grows over time, and is continually augmented by technological change—for illustrative purposes, at a total of 2.5% per year over the next several centuries. (If, instead of a constant growth rate, there is one that declines *gradually* over time, the near-term policy implications remain virtually unchanged.)

Physical capital may be increased through investment, but the effects of carbon emissions are viewed as an irreversible depletion of environmental capital. Each additional ton of cumulative carbon emissions leads to successively higher damages to the global economy.

There is a baseline emissions scenario—one that is associated with an international "do nothing" (zero abatement) policy. Such a policy might be feasible over several decades or perhaps a century, but would be unsustainable in the longer run.

To avoid ever-increasing amounts of carbon accumulation, the model includes abatement activities. They are of two types. One is characterized by increasing marginal costs and the other by constant marginal costs. The first would be typified by conservation and fuel shifting activities. It is assumed that their costs are quadratic in the amount of abatement. The second would correspond to futuristic "backstop" activities (such as photovoltaics and a hydrogen economy).

Backstops have high costs, but over the long run they are unlimited in volume, and they impose an upper bound on the long-term marginal costs of abatement. For illustrative purposes, the backstop costs are taken to be $200 per ton of carbon, and they become available in gradually increasing amounts from 2050 onward. All other technical details of the OLG model are provided in the appendix to this chapter and in a GAMS file (available upon request to the author).

ILLUSTRATIVE NUMERICAL RESULTS

Caveat: The following numerical results are illustrative, and are not intended directly for policy applications. They represent a rough composite of what has been learned in the course of Energy Modeling Forum Study 14 (integrated assessments of climate change). Their sole purpose is to demonstrate that a descriptive OLG approach can be applied to the analysis of greenhouse issues.

In examining the results from OLG, we focus upon the sensitivity of the results to the utility discount rate (udr), the annual rate at which each cohort subjectively discounts the utility of its own consumption. This rate represents the collective attitude of each age cohort toward time preference for the utility of the consumption received during its lifetime. The udr affects both the supply and the demand for investible resources.

Figure 1 shows the first and most obvious effect. Just as in an ILA model, a low udr leads to an unrealistically rapid stepup in capital formation during the early years of the planning horizon. In either an OLG or an ILA model, one of the conditions for intertemporal efficiency is that the market discount rate coincides with the consumption discount rate (cdr). With the parameters employed in this OLG model, the cdr exceeds the udr by about half a percentage point per year. (See Figure 2.) This difference equals the rate of growth of consumption by each age cohort after it has entered the labor force.

With a low udr, each cohort begins with a somewhat higher consumption level, but its consumption grows at a lower rate than with a high udr. In effect, there is an intergenerational social compact to stimulate capital formation. Figure 3 illustrates these effects for two cohorts: the one entering the labor force in the year 2000 and the one entering in 2020. Given the Cobb-Douglas form of the production function, aggregate consumption is determined largely by the assumption of a 2.5% rate of growth of the labor force (measured in efficiency units). Capital investment appears to have only a second-order impact. When the udr is varied over the range from 3% to 5%, aggregate consumption by all age cohorts in 2050 differs by only 2%.

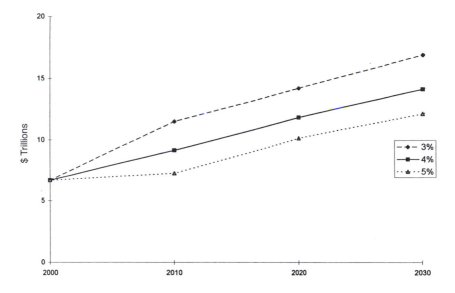

Figure 1. Aggregate Investment (Three Alternative Values of *udr*)

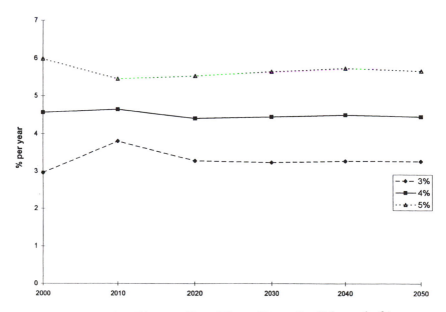

Figure 2. Consumption Discount Rate (Three Alternative Values of *udr*)

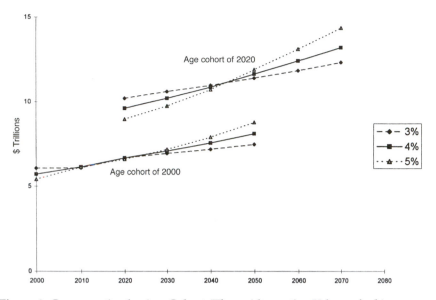

Figure 3. Consumption by Age Cohort (Three Alternative Values of *udr*)

Figures 4, 5, and 6 each have a form similar to those typically generated by ILA models. The discount rate has a major impact upon near-term abatement decisions. Figure 4 shows the price of carbon (the marginal cost of abatement). In the very long run, the price converges to the backstop cost of abatement (in this case $200 per ton). Because of short-term capacity expansion constraints, there is an intermediate phase in which the price temporarily overshoots the backstop level. During the early years of the planning horizon, the carbon price is influenced heavily by the *udr*. With a low *udr*, there is a high weight placed upon future abatement costs and future environmental impacts. It pays to engage in greater amounts of near-term abatement, and to reduce carbon emissions well below the baseline trajectory (Figure 5).

Finally, Figure 6 shows how the *udr* parameter affects the environmental capital factor, EKF. This is defined as the ratio of the world's "green" output to its conventionally measured value. The lower the value of the *udr*, the more attractive it becomes to engage in abatement, and to reduce the long-term losses in green output. Regardless of whether the *udr* is taken to be 3%, 4%, or 5%, the intertemporally efficient value of EKF lies above that associated with the do-nothing baseline emissions scenario. In each of these cases, emissions have been reduced to zero by the year 2100, the EKF remains constant thereafter, and the economy may then be described as "sustainable."

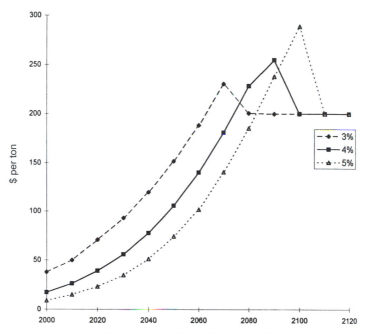

Figure 4. Carbon Price (Three Alternative Values of *udr*)

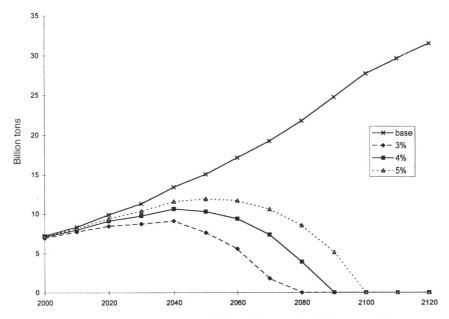

Figure 5. Carbon Emissions (Base and Three Alternative Values of *udr*)

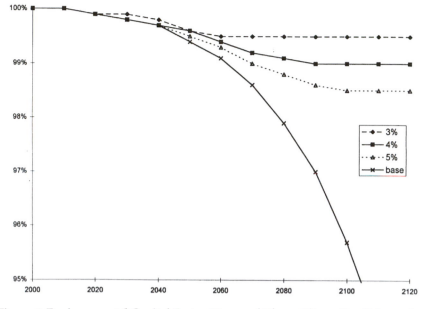

Figure 6. Environmental Capital Factor (Base and Three Alternative Values of *udr*)

There is an important consequence of the fact that EKF remains in the neighborhood of unity. This means that the value of environmental capital is a small share of total output. No matter how one assigns the ownership rights to environmental capital, the economically efficient abatement strategy is virtually unchanged. This explains the Coase-like results of the OLG model. If one were to be far more pessimistic on the damages induced by carbon emissions, one would not expect to observe this type of separation between equity and efficiency.

In parallel with the three OLG cases, it is instructive to compare an ILA formulation. All parameters and equations are identical except that now there is only a single age cohort, and its consumption is to be positive throughout the planning horizon. The single cohort's *udr* is adjusted so that the resulting market discount rate is approximately the same as that resulting from the OLG runs. It then turns out that the parallel OLG and ILA model formulations lead to virtually the identical results with respect to the variables directly relevant to greenhouse policy: carbon prices, carbon emissions, and the environmental capital factors.

Provided that the consumption discount rate is standardized between the two formulations, both the OLG and ILA results are driven by the same considerations with respect to economic efficiency. The global externalities are internalized as though the production side of the economy employed both present and future prices as a guide for decisions on investment and abatement expenditures so as to maximize the discounted value of green output that is available for consumption. The economic efficiency conditions are identical for both OLG and ILA, and equity issues may be separated from those relating to efficiency.

CONCLUSIONS

What have we learned from these numerical experiments? First, despite its simplicity, the model demonstrates the possibility of applying a descriptive approach to the logic of greenhouse gas abatement. Equity and efficiency issues may be separated. It is not essential to adopt hypotheses relating to bequest motives or to prescriptive notions of intergenerational equity. Since there is no explicit social welfare function, we can sidestep the issue of whether to discount the utility of total or of per capita consumption. All that is required is the recognition that abatement represents a specific form of capital accumulation, and that there be appropriate markets for realizing the distant-future benefits from this type of activity.

Here is an analogy. A person may buy timber lands, incur the cost of planting seedlings and subsequently benefit from the growth in the value of the tract—even though that individual does not anticipate surviving to the date of harvesting the mature trees.

Second—just as with traditional ILA analyses—the OLG model confirms the crucial role that is played by the utility discount rate. If either too low or too high a value is assigned to this parameter, there will be implausible patterns of capital formation over the near future. The *udr* has a strong influence over the rate at which consumption is discounted, and it affects both the price and quantity of greenhouse gas abatement. Alternative values of this parameter may be employed to represent alternative views on time preference for the utility of consumption.

Third, it is true that each individual has a finite life, but this has little to do with the wisdom of making investments that take a long time to pay off. Like many other ideas in economics, ILA is a convenient fiction and must not be taken too literally. At a superficial level, it sounds less realistic than OLG. At a deeper level, however, ILA provides a useful way to think through and to simplify many of the issues. It enables us to engage in the greenhouse debate without abandoning the standard tools for analyzing other forms of investments whose consequences extend over long planning horizons.

APPENDIX: TECHNICAL DESCRIPTION OF THE OLG MODEL

A Brief Literature Review

Schelling's critique indicates why it might be instructive to compare the ILA with an OLG approach. Howarth and Norgaard (1992) have applied an overlapping generations model to the economics of sustainable development, but theirs is a completely prescriptive model based on an intergenerational social welfare function. They ignore the initial distribution of labor and capital endowments between generations, and they assume that society can mandate lump-sum wealth transfers. In a number of respects, the following OLG model more nearly resembles the overlapping generations approach proposed by Auerbach and Kotlikoff (1987) for analyzing U.S. public finance issues. It is also closely related to the recursive dynamic model of global warming designed by Stephan, Mueller-Fuerstenberger, and Previdoli (1995). Their formulation examines the implications of alternative carbon taxes, but does not determine an intertemporally efficient abatement policy.

Formulation of OLG

The distinctive feature of this OLG model is that there is no motivation for bequests. To represent that idea in the simplest possible way, each age cohort has a known and finite life. It is concerned only with the discounted utility of its personal consumption during that period.

For convenience in numerical analysis, each time period is one decade in length. Each cohort lives for eight decades. During the first twenty years, there are no expenses and no income. During the next forty years, capital is accumulated from labor and capital income. During the two decades of retirement, there are consumption expenditures but no income.

The world is viewed as a closed economy in which we need not distinguish between domestic savings and investment. Year 0 refers to 2000, year 1 to 2010, and so forth. Upper-case symbols refer to decision variables, and lower-case symbols refer to parameters or to index sets. Allowing for a lag between investment and the stock available for production, and allowing for a geometric decay process of depreciation, the capital formation process may be written:

$$K_{t+1} = ksur\ K_t + 5(ksur\ I_t + I_{t+1}) \tag{1}$$

Suppose that the average life of reproducible capital is twenty years, and that $depr$ (the annual rate of depreciation) is therefore 5%. This means that *ksur* (the fraction of the capital stock or investment that survives for a decade) $= .95^{10} = .60$. Let I_0 and K_0, respectively, denote the rate of gross investment and the capital stock in the year 2000 (year 0). These are initial conditions. Thereafter, the rates of gross investment, consumption, and capital stock (respectively I_t, C_t, and K_t) are decision variables.

The labor force grows over time, and is continually augmented by technological change so that the total grows at the annual rate $g = 2.5\%$. This is sometimes described as a Harrod-neutral specification of technical change. The effective labor force in 1990 is defined as unity. Let the conventionally measured gross world product be a Cobb-Douglas function of the inputs of capital and labor. Its partial derivative with respect to K_t is the marginal productivity of capital. In a competitive economy, this represents the rate of return to capital at time t. The model is calibrated so that the annual marginal productivity of capital (net of depreciation) is 5% in 1990. For that year, the world's capital stock-output ratio is estimated at 2.8, capital's value share is 28% of the output, and the gross rate of return to capital is 10%. With a 5% rate of depreciation, the initial marginal productivity of capital is therefore 5%. Let Y_t denote the conventionally measured worldwide output in period t. Accordingly, gross output is:

$$Y_t = aK_t^{.28}L_t^{.72} \qquad (2)$$

where the scaling constant a is chosen so that the world's 1990 GDP is $23 trillion (expressed in 1990 dollars).

With a finite-horizon model, there is no easy way to avoid "edge effects." All that can be done is to verify that an extension of the horizon leads to no significant change in the decisions projected for the initial years. To reduce these boundary effects, it is stipulated that investment in the terminal year T (2200) must be sufficient to allow for depreciation and for net expansion of the capital stock at a constant geometric growth thereafter:

$$I_T = (depr + g)K_T \qquad (3)$$

Each age cohort is indexed by ac, the date at which it enters the labor force. In period t, aggregate consumption is denoted by C_t. At that time, the consumption by age cohort ac is $CC_{t,ac}$. There is positive consumption only for those age cohorts that have entered the labor force during period t itself, and during the preceding five decades. Accordingly, total consumption is written:

$$C_t = \sum_{ac=t-5}^{t} CC_{t,ac} \qquad (4)$$

Each generation's utility is based only on its own consumption stream. There is a unitary elasticity of substitution between consumption in individual time periods, and there is a constant rate at which future utilities are discounted (sometimes called the pure rate of time preference). Let this annual utility discount rate be udr, and define the ten-year utility discount factor $\beta = (1 + udr)^{-10}$. Let $udf_{t,ac}$ denote the utility discount factor applied by cohort ac to consumption in period t. For those periods in which this cohort has positive consumption, $udf_{t+1,ac} = \beta\,(udf_{t,ac})$. These utility discount factors are normalized so that their lifetime sum for each age cohort is unity. With this normalization, the $udf_{t,ac}$ factors may be interpreted as the optimal fraction of the cohort's labor and capital wealth that is expended on consumption in period t. The utility for each age cohort may therefore be written as the following product of exponentiated terms. This is a linear homogeneous function of the cohort's consumption stream:

$$\prod_t CC_{t,ac}{}^{udf_{t,ac}}$$

(where t refers only to those periods in which $CC_{t,ac} > 0$) .

An intertemporal market equilibrium is computed through a technique known as sequential joint maximization. (See Rutherford 1995.) There is one Negishi weight assigned to each age cohort, nwt_{ac}. In equilibrium, these weights represent the *share* of each cohort in the present value of global capital and labor endowments. These weights are positive and add to unity. The Negishi weights are applied to the discounted logarithms of each cohort's utility. Summing over age cohorts and restricting each cohort's utility sum to those periods in which its consumption is positive, the global Negishi maximand NWEL is as follows:

$$\text{NWEL} = \sum_{ac} nwt_{ac} \sum_t udf_{t,ac} \log(CC_{t,ac}) \tag{5}$$

We begin by assigning an arbitrary value to the Negishi weights (e.g., an egalitarian optimum in which equal values are assigned to all cohorts), and then revise them iteratively so that each agent's Negishi weight is consistent with its share of the global value of endowments. At each iteration, we solve a convex nonlinear program in which NWEL is maximized subject to constraints on conventional capital—equations (1)–(4)—and on environmental capital—equations (6)–(10) listed below. The decision variables are nonnegative. Each cohort's endowments are given, but a cohort's wealth (the total present values of these endowments) may change from one iteration to the next. The results may be interpreted as though abatement costs were financed by uniform proportional taxes on conventional capital and labor. Provided that the Negishi weights converge, this process computes an intertemporal equilibrium over all age cohorts. Convergence appears quite satisfactory for the numerical values specified here. There has been no evidence of nonuniqueness of the equilibrium.

The global environmental submodel is based upon that proposed by Olsen (1994). His work, in turn, represents a reduced-form version of the integrated assessment model reported in Manne, Mendelsohn, and Richels (1995). For his purposes, Olsen considered carbon dioxide as the only greenhouse gas. The decision variables Z_t denote global carbon emissions in period t. With no abatement efforts, Z_t will coincide with the exogenously determined baseline emissions parameters, $zbase_t$.

Abatement efforts are described by two types of decision variables, respectively, AQ_t and AB_t. The AQ_t variables describe the quantity of abatement that occurs at linearly increasing marginal costs—that is, along a quadratic cost function. The AB_t variables describe the amount of abatement that takes place at constant, but high, costs—a futuristic "backstop" activity. Global emissions are therefore:

$$Z_t = zbase_t - AQ_t - AB_t \tag{6}$$

The backstop activity will not be available until 2050. To prevent an excessively rapid rate of market penetration, it is limited to 2% of base emissions, and may not expand more than twofold during each decade thereafter. With this formulation, there is the possibility that the marginal cost of abatement may overshoot the backstop level for one or more decades after 2050. The expansion constraint is written:

$$AB_{t+1} \le .02 \, zbase_t + 2.0 \, AB_t \tag{7}$$

The decision variables ZC_t denote the quantities of carbon emitted cumulatively from 1990 onward. Because the OLG numerical projections are designed to explore the logic of the greenhouse debate, but are not intended directly for policy purposes, the model neglects atmospheric science features, such as the absorption of carbon into the biosphere and deep oceans. Emissions therefore have an irreversible effect upon atmospheric concentrations. From one decade to the next, cumulative emissions are approximated by:

$$ZC_{t+1} = ZC_t + 5(Z_{t+1} + Z_t) \tag{8}$$

Suppose that cumulative emissions lead to quadratically increasing impacts upon the economy. One way to express this idea is to define an environmental capital factor, EKF_t. This is the ratio of the world's "green" output to its conventionally measured value. Let the parameter $zcat$ denote the catastrophic cumulative emissions level at which the value of the world's green output is reduced to zero. We then have:

$$EKF_t = 1 - \left(\frac{ZC_t}{zcat}\right)^2 \tag{9}$$

According to equation (9), the EKF_t remains above 99% when ZC_t is less than 10% of $zcat$, but it rapidly approaches zero as cumulative emissions approach the catastrophic level. For purely illustrative purposes in the following numerical simulations, $zcat$ is taken to be 8000 billion tons. With this value and with the baseline emissions scenario, zero abatement implies that EKF_t remains above 99% through 2060, but drops to 95.7% by 2100. (See Figure 6.) In order to avoid this precipitous decline in EKF_t, there is an incentive to expend resources on abatement during the first half of the twenty-first century. Equation (9) can be generalized to allow for suggestions by Weitzman (1994) and others that there is a higher willingness-to-pay for the environment at high income levels. To represent this viewpoint, all that is needed is to allow for a secular decline in $zcat$.

The final set of equations provides the link between the macro and the environmental submodels of OLG. The left-hand side determines green output as the product of the environmental capital factor and the conventionally measured output derived from physical capital and labor inputs. The right-hand side represents the uses of green output: aggregate consumption, investment, and abatement costs.

$$EKF_t \, Y_t = C_t + I_t + acq_t \, AQ_t^2 + acb \, AB_t \tag{10}$$

Note that abatement costs include those that are quadratic in the amount of abatement and those that are proportional to the level of high-cost backstop activities available from 2050 onward. For illustrative purposes, the backstop costs are taken to be $200 per ton of carbon. The values of acq_t, the capital and labor endowments assigned to each age cohort, and all other technical details are listed in the GAMS file of OLG.

Necessary Conditions for a Negishi Optimal Consumption Sequence

In order to understand the numerical results of OLG, it is useful to examine the conditions that must necessarily be satisfied if a consumption sequence is to be optimal. Consider two adjacent periods (t and $t+1$) in which one age cohort's consumption is positive. Hold all parameters and decision variables constant except $CC_{t,ac}$ and $CC_{t+1,ac}$. From the Negishi maximand (5) and from the definition of the ten-year utility discount factor β, it can be seen that these two decision variables must be chosen so as to maximize:

$$\log CC_{t,ac} + \beta \log CC_{t+1,ac} \tag{11}$$

Now let π_t denote the dual variables associated with constraint (10). These measure the marginal value of green output and of consumption in each time period. Recall that aggregate consumption C_t enters only into constraints (4) and (10), and must be positive in a Negishi equilibrium. The values of the dual variables of constraints (4) and (10) will therefore be identical. In view of equation (4), these values determine the marginal rate at which the two decision variables may be traded off against each other. This means that:

$$\pi_t CC_{t,ac} + \pi_{t+1} CC_{t+1,ac} = \text{constant} \tag{12}$$

If (11) is to be maximized subject to constraint (12), a necessary condition for an intertemporal Negishi equilibrium is the following relationship governing the primal and dual variables in successive decades:

$$\frac{\pi_t}{\pi_{t+1}} = \frac{CC_{t+1,ac}}{\beta CC_{t,ac}} \tag{13}$$

Let cdr_t (the consumption discount rate) denote the annual rate of decline of the dual variables π_t. Let $ccgr_{t,ac}$ be the annual growth rate of the cohort's consumption between period t and $t+1$. With continuous compounding expressed in terms of annual rates, (13) may then be approximated by the following optimal growth condition. This applies not only in a steady state, but at all points in time:

$$cdr_t = udr + ccgr_{t,ac} \tag{14}$$

That is, for an efficient intertemporal equilibrium, the consumption discount rate must equal the sum of the utility discount rate and the rate of consumption growth by each age cohort. Note one immediate implication of equation (14). If two age cohorts have positive consumption in both periods t and $t+1$, their growth rates of consumption will be identical during this time span, and will be independent of their age. This is not necessarily consistent with the empirical evidence on lifetime consumption behavior, and it provides a reminder that many additional features would need to be added if this type of OLG were to be applied literally to the types of public finance issues studied by Auerbach and Kotlikoff (1987). For an econonometric investigation along these lines, see Attanasio and Browning (1995).

The decision variables Y_t enter only into equations (2) and (10). Accordingly, if $EKF_t = 1$ (that is, environmental losses are negligible), there would be no distinction between cdr_t and the marginal productivity of capital, the rate of decline of the dual variables associated with the production function constraints (2). In the numerical simulations described below, it turns out that the economically efficient value of EKF_t does not fall much below 98%. Accordingly, the two rates do not differ greatly from each other. To a rough approximation, the left-hand side of equation (14) may therefore be described as both the consumption discount rate and the marginal productivity of capital.

In interpreting the right-hand side of (14), one must be careful to avoid confusion between $ccgr_{t,ac}$ and g, the rate of growth of the labor force (measured in efficiency units). *Aggregate* consumption growth is largely determined by g, but each age cohort contributes to this growth in two very different ways: (a) the growth from one decade to another during its lifetime and (b) the initial level of consumption when the cohort enters into the labor market.

ACKNOWLEDGEMENTS

Thomas Schelling's provocative comments provided the initial motivation for this paper. The author owes a debt of gratitude to Gunter Stephan for a series of stimulating discussions and suggestions for revision. Helpful suggestions have also been provided by David Chang, Lawrence Goulder, Richard Richels, John Rowse, Thomas Rutherford, Joel Singer, and John Weyant. For research assistance, the author is indebted to James Deaker.

REFERENCES

Attanasio, O. P., and M. Browning. 1995. Consumption over the Life Cycle and over the Business Cycle. *American Economic Review*, 85 (5): 1118–37.

Auerbach, A., and L. Kotlikoff. 1987. *Dynamic Fiscal Policy.* Cambridge, England: Cambridge University Press.

Chichilnisky, G., and G. M. Heal. 1994. Who Should Abate Carbon Emissions? An International Viewpoint. *Economic Letters* 44: 443–49.

Cline, W. 1992. *Global Warming: The Economic Stakes.* Washington, D.C.: Institute for International Economics.

Howarth, R., and R. Norgaard. 1992. Environmental Valuation under Sustainable Development. *American Economics Association Papers and Proceedings*, 82(2): 473–77.

IPCC (Intergovernmental Panel on Climate Change). 1996. *Climate Change 1995: Economic and Social Dimensions of Climate Change*. Working Group III, the Second Assessment Report of the IPCC. Cambridge, England: Cambridge University Press.

Mäler, K.-G. 1994. Economic Growth and the Environment. In L. Pasinetti and R. Solow (eds.), *Economic Growth and the Structure of Long-Term Development*. New York: St. Martin's Press.

Manne, A., R. Mendelsohn and R. Richels. 1995. MERGE: A Model for Evaluating Regional and Global Effects of GHG Reduction Policies. *Energy Policy* 23(1): 17–34.

Nordhaus, W. 1994. *Managing the Global Commons: The Economics of Climate Change*. Cambridge, Massachusetts: MIT Press.

Olsen, T. 1994. *Greenhouse Gas Abatement: Joint Maximization under Uncertainty*. Doctoral dissertation, Department of Operations Research, Stanford University.

Peck, S., and T. Teisberg. 1992. CETA: A Model for Carbon Emissions Trajectory Assessment. *The Energy Journal* 13(1): 55–77.

Rutherford, T. 1995. *Sequential Joint Maximization*. Working paper. March. University of Colorado.

Schelling, T. 1995. Intergenerational Discounting. *Energy Policy* 23(4/5): 395–401.

Stephan, G., G. Mueller-Fuerstenberger, and P. Previdoli. 1995. *Overlapping Generations or Infinitely-Lived Agents: Designing a Framework for the Economics of Global Warming*. Working Paper 95-6. Department of Applied Micro-Economics, University of Bern.

Weitzman, M. 1994. On the "Environmental" Discount Rate. *Journal of Environmental Economics and Management* 26(1): 200–9.

13

Discounting for the Very Long Term

William R. Cline

The power of compound interest is enormous over long periods. Discounting over centuries at today's return on capital implicitly makes a commitment that is not credible: that society will keep reinvesting at this rate to compensate distant future generations for damages imposed. A much better alternative is social benefit-cost analysis applying a *social rate of time preference* (SRTP) to a stream of consumption equivalents that apply a greater than unity shadow price to capital investment effects. This approach tends to ensure that issues with time scales of centuries are not decided with severe bias against future generations. The SRTP equals the rate of pure time preference (impatience), which should be zero for social benefit-cost analysis, plus the elasticity of marginal utility multiplied by the growth rate of per capita income. This yields a discount rate of about 1.5%, except for poor economies where it may be higher. For projects with typical life spans of fifteen years, the penalty from shadow-pricing capital (for example, at 1.5 times as valuable as consumption) about neutralizes the generosity of a lower discount rate (compared with conventional rates of, say, 6% to 8%), so the method does not bias judgments toward low-return projects. For centuries-scale problems, the SRTP approach avoids the outright dismissal of future generations that occurs when conventional discount rates are used. Although I prefer systematic application of the SRTP approach, this paper proposes a compromise approach to resolve the split in the profession on this issue. The more conventional rates (without capital shadow pricing) could be applied for the first thirty years (the present generation), and the SRTP approach would then apply for all subsequent time periods.

WILLIAM R. CLINE is Deputy Managing Director and Senior Fellow at the Institute for International Finance in Washington, D.C.

My work on this subject stems from analysis of the economics of global warming (Cline 1992). Because it will take about three hundred years before deep-ocean mixing of carbon dioxide back out of the atmosphere curbs the potential rise in temperatures, this problem has a time horizon far beyond most. Time discount rates become overwhelmingly important on such time scales. For example, even with a discount rate of 5% (half the rate used in U.S. government benefit-cost analyses in the 1980s), $1 million of damage two hundred years from now shrinks to only $58 of today's discounted present value. This type of trade-off trivializes distant future effects.

I concluded it was necessary to return to basic economic theory to obtain the proper discounting method for this problem and, by implication, others such as radioactive waste disposal. Fortunately, basic theory does have a proper framework.

SOCIAL RATE OF TIME PREFERENCE (SRTP)

The literature on social benefit-cost analysis (Arrow 1966; Bradford 1975; Feldstein 1972) identifies two components for social benefit-cost analysis. First, all consumption and investment impacts should be converted to consumption equivalents by applying a shadow price to investment effects. For example, $1 worth of investment should be treated as equivalent to $1.50's worth of consumption. The concept here is that distortions in the capital market, notably including the wedge between gross and after-tax returns, cause an extra unit of investment to have a larger social value at the margin than an extra unit of consumption.

Second, the stream of consumption equivalents over time should be discounted at the SRTP. This rate is based on fundamental theory. It equals

$$\text{SRTP} = \rho + \theta g \tag{1}$$

where ρ is the rate of "pure time preference," θ is the "elasticity of marginal utility," and g is the growth rate of per capita consumption.

Pure time preference is equivalent to pure impatience: being a grasshopper instead of an ant. I agree with Ramsey (1928, 543) that it is "ethically indefensible" to discount future consumption solely because of impatience. Individually, such discounting is a recipe for living like a prince in youth but a pauper in old age. For those who take decisions on behalf of society, it is irresponsible.

That still leaves the second basis for discounting, however: we expect people to be better off in the future. If they are, then an extra dollar's consumption in the future is unlikely to be as valuable as an extra dollar's consumption today. The pace at which the incremental value from consumption falls off is called the "elasticity of marginal utility." For example, if this elasticity (θ) is 1.5, then a 10% rise in consumption causes the incremental value of an extra unit of consumption to fall by 15%. The econometric literature suggests that indeed this elasticity is in the range of one to two, although it is an admittedly elusive parameter.

Of course, discounting because people will be better off turns irrelevant if they are not going to be better off. So, the final key element is the growth rate of per capita consumption. Two centuries ago, Thomas Malthus thought this would turn to zero. So far, technological change has come to the rescue of the exhaustion of fertile soils and the diminishing returns to additional capital per worker. My best guess is that the average growth of per capita consumption over the next two to three centuries will be no more than 1% per year. That, combined with a more than doubling of global population, would multiply gross world product about 25-fold over the next three centuries. Many would argue that the earth cannot sustain such economic expansion, although I suspect it can.

The end result is that the social rate of time preference equals zero for pure impatience (ρ), plus 1.5 for the sensitivity of marginal utility to the level of consumption, multiplied by 1% for the growth rate of per capita consumption, yielding a total discount rate of 1.5% per annum. This is, of course, a much lower discount rate than is usually found in the project manuals, but it is soundly based in the theoretical literature, and it gives the distant future a fighting chance of being taken into account.[1]

CAPITAL RETURN

Opponents of the SRTP approach argue that the opportunity cost of capital should be used as the discount rate, and they cite real rates of return on capital of 6% to 8% or higher. Conceptually, the two are related, with the "wedge" of market distortions as the only difference:

$$r = \text{SRTP} + w \qquad (2)$$

where r is the rate of return on capital, and w is the wedge caused by tax and other obstacles to complete clearing of the market for capital between users in physical investment and suppliers (savers). For a centuries-long time scale, it would not be surprising to see the marginal real rates of return on capital typically at, say, 3% or lower, in view of diminishing returns to capital and, eventually, slower technological change. This would then make the SRTP at 1.5% compatible with the relation in equation (2), so long as the tax and other distortions introduce a wedge of one-half between the gross and net private return on capital. With the highest marginal U.S. income tax rate at 39% plus state taxes, a wedge of 50% is plausible.

The fundamental problem with discounting the very long term at today's rate of return on capital is that to do so makes an intergenerational comparison that promises something that cannot be delivered: that today's generation and all intervening generations will keep intact an investment fund that is capable of continued real returns at today's level, to generate a distant-future payment that will compensate a future generation for damage inflicted. This commitment is simply not credible (Arrow and others 1996; Lind and Schuler 1996). American politicians have not yet come to grips with the massive burden of Medicare and social security that a relatively smaller workforce will have to shoulder just two or three decades from now. If we are this bad at planning for thirty years, how can we possibly believe a commitment that somehow society will invest over two to three centuries (at today's rate of return) in a sort of "fund for future greenhouse victims" or "future radioactive waste victims" without fear that in the interim some populist administration will loot the fund? Because this commitment cannot be counted on, because the rates of return cannot be counted on, and because it is not even clear that there is a meaningful vehicle for storing this physical investment in a way that will generate goods and services relevant to the generation two centuries from now, discounting at today's rate of return on capital seems highly likely to stack the cards against future generations. This leaves the social rate of time preference as a far superior approach.

Equation (2) also illustrates one of the points critics of the SRTP approach like to make: that there would need to be a massive program of saving and investment to drive down the rate of return on capital (r) to equal SRTP, rather than SRTP $+ w$. However, this is not an argument against undertaking politically feasible projects that pass the SRTP test, but rather an argument that there may be a need for greater political education to make feasible other projects that also pass this test but that the public is currently unwilling to undertake. The fact that some higher return projects exist but have been politically rejected should not block action in such areas as greenhouse abatement if the political will is present for the latter, and action passes the test of social benefit-cost analysis.

EMPATHIC DISTANCE

Schelling (1993) argues that because Americans do not presently care much about the poor in developing countries, as revealed by aid budgets, neither do they care about their own descendants in the distant future. The two sets of people are, by his interpretation, both comparably distant in terms of present-day Americans' empathy. He thus sees little basis for accepting present costs to avoid damage to distant future generations.

We have a recent empirical test that would seem to reject this proposition of intertemporal-intercountry symmetry. President Clinton just set aside a large block of southern Utah on behalf of America's future generations. Can you imagine his having instead turned it over to Bangladesh for strip mining? Yet, according to Schelling's symmetry theory, Clinton should have been indifferent between these alternatives.[2]

PRESCRIPTIVE VERSUS DESCRIPTIVE?

To keep the peace with my coauthors in the recent chapter on discounting in the 1996 economic report of the Intergovernmental Panel on Climate Change (Arrow and others 1996), I went along uncomfortably with the dichotomy of "prescriptive" to denote the social rate of time preference approach outlined earlier and "descriptive" to denote either the use of capital return for discounting or the use of optimization models that apply a pure time preference rate (ρ) of 3% or more rather than zero.[3] Although the classification did correctly call attention to a split in the profession, it is misleading if interpreted loosely as "hypothetical" or "normative" versus "actual" or "positive," as some might do. In particular, the best empirical (hence descriptive) estimate for the risk-free rate at which savers can transfer consumption into the future is surely the real rate of return on treasury bills. Yet, this real rate is historically close to zero, not the 3% or more that some members of the "descriptive" club apply for pure time preference (impatience).

DIFFERENT METHODS FOR DIFFERENT PROJECTS?

But doesn't the social rate of time preference approach for long-term environmental projects imply different discount approaches for different projects? No. The approach is general. The specific rates that emerge from the approach can vary, however.

In a low-income country, the elasticity of marginal utility (θ) may be high, because at low incomes marginal utility may be extremely high but drop off rapidly as income rises. Similarly, the growth rate (g) may be high, from a low base. So, it is not implausible that the social rate of time preference appropriate for the country may approximate the 6%–8% range that might also be alternatively reached using the capital return approach.

However, it must be kept in mind that the social benefit-cost approach not only applies the SRTP but also imposes a shadow-price expansion of capital costs. As a result, the approach is far from being a device for justifying low-return projects. Consider an industrial country where the SRTP is 1.5%, as outlined earlier. For a project with a single initial investment that generates a fifteen-year stream of constant annual consumption benefits (and no salvage value), conventional discounting at 8% yields exactly the same result as discounting at the SRTP of 1.5% combined with applying a shadow price of 1.56 units of consumption per unit of capital to the initial investment.[4] Those who equate social benefit-cost analysis using the SRTP approach with a bias toward low-return projects (apparently including Birdsall and Steer 1993) thus miss the point.

The more fundamental consideration is that whereas the social benefit-cost approach can generate results quite similar to those of conventional discounting over a period of ten to twenty years, for time scales of centuries the difference can be enormous because the power of the discount rate grows exponentially with time, swamping the shadow price applied to the initial investment.

ENVIRONMENTAL PRICING

Environmental pricing means that what is unique about environmental projects is not that they should be given a low discount rate because they are environmental, but, instead, that they may wind up with low discount rates because they have extremely long time horizons. If a particular environmental project will run out of benefits in a few years because it is strictly a temporary cleanup, the issues of this seminar do not really arise.

However, proper environmental pricing is challenging even on a short horizon, and becomes more so as the horizon lengthens. Valuing human life for projects that affect mortality is among the most contentious, especially when both rich and poor countries are involved. For projects with long-horizon consequences, it is necessary to consider the likely path of the price of the environmental good relative to goods and services generally. One would expect this relative price to be rising, both because of finite supply and because environmental services are income elastic (hence, the so-called Kuznets curve for pollution, showing first a rise and then a decline as per capita income rises and countries devote more resources to a clean environment). Again, however, proper pricing of the environmental effects is a separable issue from time discounting. Thus, the rising relative price of environmental services would seem to be the most straightforward way to ensure against Sen's (1982) "tyranny" of the present generation over a richer but environmentally deprived future generation.

TOWARD A WORKABLE COMPROMISE FOR
INTERGENERATIONAL DISCOUNTING

The SRTP approach described earlier does not explicitly distinguish between intra- and intergenerational discounting. It winds up with relatively low discount rates for the latter primarily because over such a long horizon, the plausible growth rate and elasticity of marginal utility parameters yield that outcome. In contrast, there is a more radical tradition regarding very long-term discounting that contends there should be no discounting at all of effects on future generations, because they do not yet exist and cannot participate in the decisions in question (Mishan 1975). This same notion that "future generations are different" is also present in Schelling's empathic distance, albeit with just the opposite outcome.

As reviewed by Arrow and others (1996), there exists a sharp divide among economists who have examined this issue, between the groups labeled "descriptive" and "prescriptive" as noted earlier. Let me propose a compromise.

Suppose we take as the point of departure the notion that there is an important distinction between the future generation and the present generation. Suppose we denote one generation as thirty years. Then, a workable compromise could be that the SRTP approach is applied *at least* after the first thirty years. The method applied for economic effects that take place in the first thirty years would ideally also be SRTP but, under the compromise approach, could acceptably be capital opportunity cost and/or optimization with some significant pure time preference ($\rho > 0$) during this initial period. This phasing adheres to the descriptive school, because financial markets effectively do not extend beyond thirty years, so there is nothing to be described in the longer period.

As an illustration, suppose that one accepted from the descriptionist school that for the first thirty years the rate of pure time preference is 3%, and in an optimization model with a usual utility function (such as logarithmic), and under conditions of, say, 2% per capita growth, the discount rate would be 5%. Then, the descriptionists could have 5% discounting for the first thirty years. The prescriptionist-SRTP school would then have, say, 1.5% discounting of all effects occurring in subsequent years, *with the discounting for this period starting from a base of the first year rather than the values already shrunken by descriptionist discounting in the first thirty years.*

Figure 1 shows the resulting profile of this compromise discounting procedure. The vertical axis shows the discounted present value of a unit of consumption received at the year along the horizontal axis. All consumption-equivalent effects in the first thirty years are discounted at 5% (in this example) and in the following years at 1.5%. The resulting time path of the present discounted value of unity would follow the

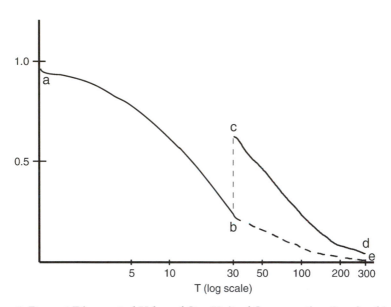

Figure 1. Present Discounted Value of One Unit of Consumption Received in Year *T*.

curve *abcd*. The intellectual justification for the break at thirty years is that this is a generational break, and, in addition, that this demarcates a horizon that actual financial markets reach. There is, of course, the resulting discontinuity that one real dollar received in Year 30 is worth only twenty-three cents [$= 1/(1.05)^{30}$], whereas one real dollar received in Year 31 is worth more: sixty-three cents [$= 1/(1.015)^{31}$]. It would, however, violate both the intergenerational consideration and the spirit of the descriptionist-prescriptionist compromise to begin the lower discounting path from values already discounted in the first thirty years at the higher rate (turning the discounted present value path into *abe*).

An important part of the compromise approach would be that if broadly conventional discount rates are used in the first thirty years (for example, a capital opportunity cost of 6%–8% real), then all capital investment costs in this period would be accounted at their face value, rather than expanded by a shadow price on capital as in the social benefit-cost, SRTP approach. As noted earlier, the resulting estimates would not necessarily be very different between the two approaches in at least the first decade or two.

The practical effect of this compromise approach for most projects with centuries-scale impact horizons would be close to that of outright application of the SRTP approach for the whole period. A major feature of these cases tends to be that abatement today generates a small annual stream of benefits that grows over time and persists into the very distant future, with abatement costs conversely concentrated toward the beginning of the period. The bulk of the benefits of abatement in such cases would thus have the same discounting in the compromise approach as in the strict SRTP approach over the whole horizon.

At the same time, this compromise approach would tend to recognize the emphasis many in the descriptionist school place on phased rather than instantaneous action. For example, the compromise approach would tend to favor phasing investment costs toward the end of the first thirty-year period (but no later), whereas application of the SRTP uniformly across the thirty-year period and after would tend to push investment costs more toward the initial years because there would be less cost shrinkage from initial delay. For problems with centuries-scale consequences, a delay limited to five or ten years is not fatal, especially if there is further justification from evolving scientific knowledge. Insofar as greater delay had greater future damages (for example, avoiding greenhouse abatement until Year 29), these greater damages would show up in a proper analysis of benefits and costs, tending to push the action back toward the beginning of the horizon.

CONCLUSION

The power of compound interest is enormous over long periods. Economists have sophisticated approaches that can deal with the special challenges raised by environmental and other issues that have time horizons on the order of centuries rather than a few years. For decisions on such issues, it is incumbent on economists to go beyond application of their business-as-usual discounting formulas that were designed for projects with horizons of at most two or three decades.

ENDNOTES

[1]Identification of the proper shadow price on capital in this method is tricky and has generated a literature that has had explosive rather than sensible conclusions because of assumptions of what the government does with the resources generated by the project. Based on a return to a more straightforward definition of this shadow price, I estimate that it is likely to be in the range of 1.5 to 2 (Cline 1992, 274).

[2]There is also an ironical implication of Schelling's approach. Essentially it says that the elasticity of marginal utility is zero when applied interpersonally rather than to a single person. Rich Americans are unwilling to redistribute anything to poor Bangladeshis (or, for that matter, poor Americans), implying that there is equal marginal utility for rich and poor and thus that $\theta = 0$. Yet, if we

apply this parameter to the SRTP approach, we would get SRTP = 0 [equation (1)]. Empathic distance would ironically generate a zero rate of long-term discount, rather than a high rate.

[3]As an example of the latter approach within this school, see Nordhaus (1994).

[4]If c is the annual consumption generated, and K is the initial capital outlay, if $K = \Sigma_{t=1,15}c/(1.08)^t$ then $1.56K = \Sigma_{t=1,15}c/(1.015)^t$.

REFERENCES

Arrow, Kenneth J. 1966. Discounting and Public Investment Criteria. In A. V. Kneese and S. C. Smith (eds.), *Water Research*. Baltimore: Johns Hopkins University Press for Resources for the Future, 13–32.

Arrow, Kenneth J., William R. Cline, Karl-Göran Mäler, Mohan Munasinghe, Ray Squitieri, and Joseph E. Stiglitz. 1996. Intertemporal Equity, Discounting, and Economic Efficiency. In J. P. Bruce, H. Lee, and E. F. Haites (eds.), *Climate Change 1995: Economic and Social Dimensions of Climate Change*. Cambridge: Cambridge University Press, 128–44.

Birdsall, Nancy, and Andrew Steer. 1993. Act Now on Global Warming—But Don't Cook the Books. *Finance and Development* 30(1): 6–8.

Bradford, David F. 1975. Constraints on Government Investment Opportunities and the Choice of Discount Rate. *American Economic Review* 65(5, December): 887–99.

Cline, William R. 1992. *The Economics of Global Warming*. Washington, D.C.: Institute for International Economics.

Feldstein, Martin S. 1972. The Inadequacy of Weighted Discount Rates. In Richard Layard (ed.), *Cost Benefit Analysis*. Middlesex, England: Penguin Books, 311–32.

Lind, Robert, and Richard Schuler. 1996. *Equity and Discounting*. NBER-Yale Conference on Economics and Policy Issues in Global Warming. July 23–24, 1996, Snowmass, Colorado.

Mishan, E. J. 1975. *Cost Benefit Analysis: An Informal Introduction*. London: Allen & Unwin.

Nordhaus, W. 1994. *Managing the Global Commons: The Economics of Climate Change*. Cambridge, Massachusetts: MIT Press.

Ramsey, Frank P. 1928. A Mathematical Theory of Saving. *Economic Journal* 138(152): 543–59.

Schelling, Thomas C. 1993. Intergenerational Discounting. College Park: University of Maryland. Mimeographed.

Sen, Amartya K. 1982. Approaches to the Choice of Discount Rates for Social Benefit-Cost Analysis. In Robert Lind (ed.), *Discounting for Time and Risk in Energy Policy*. Washington, D.C.: Resources for the Future.

14

Models and Discount Rates

Comments on Manne and Cline

Shantayanan Devarajan

If the job of a discussant is to generate a discussion, then my task is an easy one, since the papers by Alan Manne and William Cline disagree with one another. I should just step out of the way, ask each author to address the other's paper, and we will have a lively exchange. However, my task is also a difficult one because I have problems with both papers, although some of those problems may not be germane to the question of this workshop, namely, how should very long-term projects be discounted? In what follows, therefore, I will comment on the two papers individually but try to point out some connections between them so that we may make some progress in answering the fundamental question of this workshop.

ALAN MANNE'S PAPER

The question of how very long-term projects, especially those associated with mitigating climate change, should be discounted is itself really two questions: What *principle* should be used to determine the discount rate? What should the *level* of the discount rate be? Alan Manne's paper (Chapter 12) concentrates on the former while, as we will see, William Cline's paper (Chapter 13) is devoted almost exclusively to the latter question.

The Manne paper makes the correct point that it *is* possible to separate efficiency from equity issues in intertemporal decisionmaking. The

SHANTAYANAN DEVARAJAN is Research Manager for Public Economics in the Development Research Group of the World Bank.

efficiency issue has to do with the public-goods nature of carbon abatement (or the public "bads" nature of climate change). Equity is not an issue that is intrinsic to climate change; the intergenerational wealth transfers we are discussing are for efficiency reasons.

At the same time, it could be argued that this separation of equity and efficiency issues is artificial, that it is a construct of the underlying model, which is that of a representative, infinitely lived agent (ILA). Quite simply, since there is only one agent, by definition there can be no discussion of equity issues. Alan correctly questions whether the ILA model is the appropriate one for discussing climate-change and other very long-run problems. He quotes Tom Schelling as saying they are "inappropriate" and proceeds to consider an alternative—the overlapping generations (OLG) framework. The OLG model is the polar opposite of the ILA model in its treatment of intergenerational altruism. Unlike the ILA framework in which the agent cares about every future date, in the OLG model, no one cares about the future beyond the two periods in which he or she lives. Alan asks whether an OLG model will give significantly different results from his standard ILA computable general equilibrium model.

The answer is that the OLG and ILA models give almost identical results in terms of intergenerational allocations. This is an intriguing outcome, especially given the very different perspectives of the two models. Unfortunately, the models are a bit too complicated to explain the intuition behind why the outcomes are so similar. To assist in the latter, I will present an extremely simple OLG model with an exhaustible resource (developed in collaboration with my colleague Heng-fu Zou). The model will help us understand why an OLG model may give results that are similar to an ILA model.

An OLG Model with an Exhaustible Resource

Each generation lives for two periods. They work in Period 1 by extracting an amount α of the resource (the total stock of the resource is one). They consume some of this income and buy coupons (M) with the rest. In the second period, they sell their coupons to finance their consumption. In symbols, the tth generation's problem (assuming logarithmic utility) is to

$$\text{Max} \log C_t^1 + \beta \log C_t^2 \text{ s.t.}$$

$$P_t C_t^1 + M_t^1 = \alpha_t$$

$$P_{t+1} C_t^2 = M_t^1$$

$$C_t^1 + C_{t-1}^2 = \alpha_t$$

$$1 \geq \Sigma \alpha_t$$

where subscripts refer to the generation and superscripts to the year of their lives (one is when they are young and two, when they are old); β is the discount factor.

In this setup, it is natural to ask why one generation does not consume all of the resource. That is, why is α not equal to one for, say, the tth generation? If we solve the tth generation's optimization problem, we obtain the following condition:

$$\left(\frac{1+\beta}{P_t} \right) (\alpha_{t-1} + \beta \alpha_t) = \alpha_{t-1} \alpha_t^2$$

Now, if generation $(t-1)$ decided to consume all of the resource, that would leave $\alpha_t = 0$. In that case, the left-hand side of the foregoing condition would also need to equal zero, meaning that P_t would approach infinity. But, this would mean that members of the $(t-1)$th generation would starve in their old age, since as P_t approached infinity, C_{t-1}^2 would approach zero. Thus, it is not in the interest of members of generation $(t-1)$ to extract all of the resource, even though they have no desire to leave any of it for future generations. The key is the overlapping nature of the generations and the fact that members of the older generation rely on the young to provide the goods that they can buy with their coupons.

While this simple model indicates why an OLG framework will not lead to an environmental disaster, it does not explain why Manne's ILA and OLG results are numerically so close. The answer there probably lies in the similarity of the first-order conditions of his two models. But, the basic intuition as to why, if we depart quite radically from the ILA model, the resulting intergenerational allocation may still be a reasonable one can be gleaned from the simple OLG model described earlier.

WILLIAM CLINE'S PAPER

Although he arrives at very different discount rates from Alan Manne, William Cline's paper is firmly in the ILA tradition. Indeed, Cline does not reject the basic principles of discounting that result from the ILA model. The formula he applies follows directly from the model. What he does not like are the actual numbers that emerge when the formula is applied. Cline's paper then is an attempt to choose values for various unobservable parameters in the formula until it generates some reasonable values for the social discount rate.

There are several problems with this approach. First, the actual value of a discount rate is dependent on the choice of numeraire. It is difficult to say a priori whether 5% is a high or low number for a discount rate unless we specify the numeraire and show how it compares with other trajectories with that same numeraire. Second, since the discount rate is the rate of decrease of the price of the numeraire good, it is part of the dual to the primal optimal solution of an allocation problem. In that case, I am very uncomfortable with changing the value of the discount rate (by varying certain parameters) without knowing how this changes the primal optimal solution. Put another way, I would like to see the underlying model (and its optimal solution) that gives rise to the particular path of the discount rate preferred by Cline. As we have seen at this workshop, different models can give rise to very different paths of the discount rate—but it is important to understand what those models are. Third, Cline bases much of his argument on the notion that the pure rate of time preference is or should be zero, and this permits him to arrive at a much lower social discount rate than others have. However, Alan Manne's paper describes a reasonable climate-change scenario, including considerable abatement in the optimal solution, with pure rates of time preference of 3%–5%. So, while Cline may object to the social discount rate implicit in Manne's model, does he also object to the climate-change scenario that is consistent with that social discount rate?

The general issue is whether the debate should focus solely on the numerical value of the social discount rate. Climate change clearly involves some efficiency problems. As with all efficiency problems, we should be developing subsidies and taxes to address them. Once these subsidies and taxes are in place, the discount rate will come out in the wash. Thus, we may be better off concentrating on the primal solution, rather than discussing numerical values of the dual.

15

Discounting and Public Policies That Affect the Distant Future

William D. Nordhaus

A discount rate is a price used to compare future and present goods. This paper addresses the following issue: When the implications of conventional benefit-cost tests are ethically unacceptable, how might they be modified? I examine this question by employing different rules in an empirical model of global warming. The major conclusion is that ad hoc manipulation of discount rates is a very poor substitute for policies that focus directly on the ultimate objective. Moreover, within the class of policies that distort discount rates, targeted distortions in the specific sectors are less harmful than distortions of discount rates in the entire economy. The best approach will generally be to identify the long-term objective and to directly override market decisions or conventional benefit-cost tests to achieve the ultimate goals. Focusing on ultimate objectives shows trade-offs explicitly, makes the cost of violating benefit-cost rules transparent, and allows public decisionmakers to weigh options explicitly rather than allowing technicians to hide the choices in abstruse arguments.

INTRODUCTION

Important issues that affect the distant future pose deep difficulties for public policy. Some obstacles are political, such as getting elected officials with two-year electoral cycles to focus on problems beyond their election horizons. Other issues are complicated by intractable uncertainties about

WILLIAM D. NORDHAUS is A. Whitney Griswold Professor of Economics at Yale University.

what the world will look like in a century or more. But at a deeper level, it is apparent that our conventional tools of economic analysis are poorly designed to deal with long-term investments. Like distant objects reduced by the perspective of space, distant economic events are diminished by discounting to such tiny magnitudes that they become negligible in the standard economic benefit-cost calculus. The question I address is, what are effective ways to tackle important long-term issues that are discounted to epsilons in treatments that use conventional discounting techniques?

I will take as an example of this syndrome the issue posed by long-term global warming. This problem is examined because the dilemmas involved in global warming are relatively well understood and can usefully serve as a metaphor for the issues involved in public policies that balance economic needs with longer-term social or environmental objectives. In addition, among all the variables, the discount rate has the largest impact on current policy for global warming. It is not surprising, therefore, that no economic question has caused more confusion and controversy in this area than that of the appropriate discount rate.

In this contribution, I do not intend to review the different philosophical and theoretical arguments concerning discounting—these are well known and have been well argued for many years. Rather, I propose to investigate the impact of different approaches on the ultimate outcomes—on consumption and climate-change trajectories. For this purpose, I use a simple calibrated growth model that includes a stock global environmental public good. I stipulate at the beginning that conventional benefit-cost analyses may give results that are unacceptable. The question is, what is a useful and efficient approach to overriding conventional techniques?

BACKGROUND ON DISCOUNT RATES

It is easy to lose sight of the fact that discount rates are only prices. That is, a discount rate is a relative price used to compare future and present goods and services in benefit-cost analyses. A little background will elucidate this point.

Begin with some crucial terms of art. In what follows, a *discount rate* is a pure number per unit of time that allows us to convert values in the future into values today. The conventional use of the discount rate applies to the *discount rate on goods and services*, which applies to bundles of goods in the marketplace at different times. Underlying judgments about the relative importance of utilities or well-being over time are contained in the *pure rate of time preference*, which represents the relative weights on the welfare of generations measured in terms of the rate at which we discount the well-being of future generations relative to the well-being of the current generation. A well-known result of optimal growth theory is that if we maximize the discounted utility of consumption of a stationary population in an economy without distortions, the discount rate on goods and services should equal the real interest rate. The real interest rate, in turn, should equal the pure rate of social time preference plus the rate of growth of per capita consumption times a parameter that reflects the degree to which we are averse to inequality among different generations.

The conventional economic approach to the design of public policies is to use benefit-cost analysis. Under this approach, the increments to consumption—of different goods and services, in different regions, at different times, with different risk profiles, and in different uncertain states of the world—are evaluated at the appropriate shadow prices applying to those increments. When the distribution of consumption across individuals is appropriate and when there are no distortions, then the appropriate shadow prices for competitively produced private goods (or appropriately internalized public goods) are their market prices.

This general principle applies to the pricing of goods over time as well as over other dimensions. Assuming the idealized conditions of the last paragraph, the appropriate price to use in discounting future goods and services would be the real rate of return on investment over the relevant time horizon. This approach has been called the "descriptive approach" because it uses real returns in the marketplace as the discount rate or price for goods in much the same way that benefit-cost analyses conventionally use the market price of land, wheat, oil, labor, or risk in evaluating decisions that involve changes in these variables. Table 1 shows a recent compilation of estimates of the real return on investment in different sectors and countries. I do not see how anyone who looks at these data could convince themselves that the real rate of return on investment is currently below 6% annually on a post-tax basis.[1]

While the economic logic of using the market price for the discount rate is powerful, there are cases where the implications of that technique are questionable or unacceptable. An important example, and one that applies to the issue addressed here, concerns discounting of the distant future. It is clear that if we use a realistic market discount rate on goods, future conditions will receive little weight. The U.S. government has mandated that a real discount rate on goods of 7% per year be used in government investment decisions. At this rate, $1,000 of damages will be valued at only $1.15 in 100 years and at $0.0013 in 200 years. Private sector discount rates on goods are likely to be even higher. It is true that catastrophic outcomes (with utility costs approaching $-\infty$) will still have high negative present value, but routine risks will be discounted away.

Table 1. Rates of Return on Investment.

Asset class	Period	Real rate of return (percent per year)
All private capital, U.S.		
Pre-tax	1963–85	5.7
Corporate capital, U.S.		
Post-tax		
All corporations	1963–85	5.7
Large firms	1963–85	6.1
Pre-tax, large firms	1963–85	12.3
Human capital		
United States	1980s	6–12
Developing countries		
Primary education	Various	26
Secondary education	Various	16
Higher education	Various	13
Consumer investments		
Ten studies	1976–88	
Mean		68.0
Median		48.5
Energy conservation		
Thirteen studies	1978–88	
Mean		22.6
Median		19.5
Nonresidential capital stock, G-7 countries	1975–90	15.1

Note: This table shows a compilation of estimates of the real (inflation-corrected) rate of return on investments in different sectors. This is drawn from William D. Nordhaus, *Managing the Global Commons*, MIT Press, 1994.

The following hypothetical example might illustrate the issue. Suppose that scientists discover an asteroid on a 200-year orbit that will shortly pass by the Earth. Calculations reveal that on the next orbit, which will occur in 200 years, the asteroid will hit and destroy Florida. We can push the asteroid off course today by launching a missile with conventional explosives, rendering the asteroid harmless forever. What would a conventional benefit-cost analysis recommend? The current value of land and capital in Florida is approximately $2 trillion. Using the mandated 7% discount rate on goods, we find that preventing Florida from evaporating in 200 years would be worth only $3 million today. Therefore, if the missile launch costs more than $3 million, current procedures would advise against saving Florida. (Readers with no particular fondness for Florida could just as easily substitute New York City, northern California, or the Netherlands, and the numbers would be approximately the same.)

Whatever the economic logic, using the conventional discount rate on goods in such cases violates our ethical intuition. We often make decisions that are not economical—whether because of a sense of place or justice or religious conviction. Benefit-cost analysis would tell us that it is economical to expose the populations in the distant future to significant radiation risks from nuclear waste sites, but current practice is not to discount future radiation risks at all. Similarly, we might choose not to use a conventional discounting approach to estimate the value of protecting Venice or Florida from a rising sea level, the value of a stand of redwoods that would take one thousand years to regenerate, or the value of a site like Yellowstone National Park that is a unique geological treasure. Of course, to say that we might question the results of a straight discount-rate-based benefit-cost analysis does not mean that we would protect Venice or Yellowstone or a stand of redwoods at any cost. Rather, it means that we might want to ask whether the benefits of certain long-term objectives are worth the (excess) costs.

The basic point is that conventional benefit-cost analyses are rules of thumb for decisionmaking. They simplify calculations and reduce the dimensionality of a problem. But they cannot substitute for judgment. When the implications of the calculations are ethically unacceptable, or where the underlying assumptions are questionable, we must step back and ask whether there are implicit assumptions in the decision criterion that are flawed.

When calculations involving discount rates on goods compare the return on items that are subject to numerous comparable decisions or investments (market consumption today with market consumption in the future), then we must be careful to ensure that we use comparable "prices" or decision criteria lest we engage in inefficient activities. Often, however, the decisions involve items which are not comparable to other private-sector or even public-sector decisions. Consider social decisions such as whether or not to establish Yellowstone National Park, to expose the distant future to radiation, to allow the extinction of blue whales or smallpox, or to allow massive climate change. These activities are not ones where a robust set of private markets or public decisions can be used to compare the trade-offs with respect to current consumption. Sometimes, a society may decide that such activities are intrinsically important in a way that cannot be captured by market valuations. It is here that we may need to supplement or override conventional benefit-cost tests or conventional discount rates on goods.

Are there simple rules for overriding conventional benefit-cost tests? I will conclude here that there are no magic formulas. In what follows, I will examine the impact of using different criteria for overriding a conventional discounted benefit-cost test. That is, in the context of global warming, I will examine the economic costs and environmental benefits of certain policies that have been proposed as a way of supplanting a standard discounted benefit-cost analysis. By their nature, these policies will be second-best approaches and will be inefficient in the sense that they lower the discounted value of the utility of consumption. What I am seeking is to determine which alternative approaches are *relatively efficient* in attaining certain environmental objectives.

MODELING DETAILS (DICE MODEL)

In the examples that follow, I will investigate different approaches using an economic model of global warming called the DICE model, which is an acronym for a Dynamic Integrated model of Climate and the Economy[2] This model integrates the economic costs and benefits of greenhouse gas (GHG) reductions with a simple dynamic representation of the scientific links of emissions, concentrations, and climate change. The DICE model is designed to choose levels of investment in tangible capital and in GHG reductions that maximize a social welfare function. The social welfare function is the discounted sum of the utilities of per capita consumption times population. The emphasis is on intertemporal choice, where there is in every period a choice between current consumption, investment in reproducible capital, and GHG abatement. The version presented here considers an aggregate global economy and considers only the intertemporal choice issue, ignoring issues of income inequality across countries. The model is calibrated to major economic and climate-change variables and operates for an indefinitely long period with time steps of ten years. Modeling details are presented in the technical appendix to this paper.

The baseline run assumes a constant rate of pure time preference of 3% per year. This generates a real interest rate and a net marginal productivity of capital that start around 6% per year and decline slowly to the pure rate of time preference as population and per capita income stabilize. The discount rate on goods is chosen to be consistent with observed returns on capital, or revealed social time preference, although if anything it errs on the side of being too low a discount rate on goods. (See Table 1 for some representative data.) The DICE model has been through many variants, and its main sensitivity is to the pure rate of time preference.

ALTERNATIVE APPROACHES

Consider an "efficient" economic program—one that optimizes the posited social welfare function.[3] It should be emphasized that this "optimal" climate change is one in which marginal costs and benefits of emissions are balanced. In the global warming context, the "optimal" policy involves mitigation costs of around $10 billion annually in the near term rising to $50 billion after a couple of centuries.

Even with this large expenditure, the long-run global average temperature rises sharply. After 500 years, it increases 6.16 °C (11.1 °F) over the 1900 global climate. While we have only the foggiest idea of what this would imply in terms of ecological, economic, and social outcomes, it would make most thoughtful people nervous to induce such a large environmental change. We might decide that this "efficient" economic program is unacceptable, just as we might think it worth more than $3 million today to prevent Florida from being inundated in 200 years.

How might we then redesign our policies? I will analyze four different approaches.

Raise Savings or Lower the Overall Discount Rate

One approach—which seems to be the idea behind the so-called prescriptive approach—rests on the argument that discount rates on goods that are actually used in markets are too high to be ethically justifiable. Society should therefore take policies to implement a lower and ethically justifiable rate of time preference. This would imply that society would increase its savings rate sufficiently to drive the return to capital and the discount rate on goods down to ethically justifiable levels. This would also drive down the discount rate on global warming investments and lower long-run climate change.

The precise alternative policy examined here is to choose savings rates and climate policies consistent with rates of time preference of 0% and 1% per annum rather than 3% per annum. The consumption profiles generated by this policy are then evaluated using the 3% rate of time preference.

Differential Discounting

A second approach might be sensible where the discount rate on goods was felt to be too high but society could not generate the political will to reduce consumption and lower the overall discount rate on goods. This approach would apply especially low discount rates to a certain class of projects. These might be ones with extremely long payoffs or ones in preferred ethical habitats, such as the environment. In this case, conventional investments would continue to have the normal high discount rate on goods, but the favored sectors would use the low discount rate for investments.

The policies examined here are to choose climate-change policies that are consistent with pure rates of social of time preference of 0% and 1%

per annum, while recognizing that conventional investments will continue to be made at the normal discount rate on goods.

Climate Targeting

A third approach sets certain long-run objectives in terms of the ultimate variable of interest, in this case the environmental variable. For example, it might be decided that total climate change should not exceed a given temperature target.

I take a wide range of temperature limitations for this policy, ranging from a ceiling of 2 °C to one of 5.5 °C.

Emission or Concentration Limitations

A final approach—which has been widely advocated in climate negotiations—is to target an intermediate variable, such as GHG emissions or concentrations. The Framework Convention on Climate Change (FCCC), for example, holds that GHG concentrations should be kept below "dangerous levels." As a matter of policy, the FCCC endorses limiting emissions to 1990 levels. The Kyoto Protocol of December 1997 assigns emission reductions to "Annex I" countries, with the 2010 emission reductions targeted to average 6% of 1990 levels for the group.

The two sets of policies investigated here are emission limitations at 100% and 80% of global 1990 emissions, and concentration limits at 150%, 200%, and 300% of 1990 levels of CO_2-equivalent concentrations of GHGs.

Each of the four approaches has its shortcomings. Each is inefficient (if we have correctly modeled the underlying preferences). All of them are suboptimal for the hypothesized social welfare function. *The question we address is level of inefficiency as well as the long-term environmental gain.*

RESULTS OF THE MODELING

Table 2 and Figures 1a and 1b show the basic results. Table 2 provides the basic data on the outcomes.

The figures are the most useful for interpreting the results. These show the trade-off between the reduction in annualized world income on the horizontal axis and the long-term climate change on the vertical axis. Annualized income is calculated as the annualized difference in the present value of utility between the reference path and the "optimal" path; I have put utility into first-period consumption equivalence and annualized by multiplying the present value by an annualization factor (here

Table 2. Basic Results for Alternative Policies.

Policy	Policy parameter	Rate of time preference (percent per annum)		Difference in annualized income (billions of 1990 $)	Initial values of key variables		Temperature change (°C) +500 years
		Utility	Environment		Emission control rate	Carbon tax ($/tC)	
Market	No controls	0.03	0.03	-1.9	0.000	0.0	6.55
Optimal		0.03	0.03	0.0	0.088	5.2	6.16
High saving (low overall discount rate)		0.01	0.01	-142.8	0.196	22.7	5.58
		0.00	0.00	-230.4	0.404	92.7	4.36
Differential discount rate		0.03	0.01	-4.5	0.192	22.7	5.58
		0.03	0.00	-37.2	0.217		4.36
Climate target	T change < 5.5	0.03	NA	0.0	0.088	5.2	5.50
	T change < 5	0.03	NA	-0.1	0.088	5.3	5.00
	T change < 4	0.03	NA	-2.5	0.910	5.6	4.00
	T change < 3	0.03	NA	-23.5	0.012	9.5	3.00
	T change < 2	0.03	NA	-127.8	0.261	40.8	2.00
Emission limitation	E < E(1990)	0.03	NA	-52.6	0.137	12.0	3.43
	E < 0.8 E(1990)	0.03	NA	-202.2	0.272	46.4	3.05
Concentration limitation	M < 1.5 × M(0)	0.03	NA	-106.1	0.088	38.1	2.43
	M < 2 × M(0)	0.03	NA	-17.1	0.112	8.2	3.47
	M < 3 × M(0)	0.03	NA	-0.3	0.252	5.3	4.91

Note: Table shows the basic results for the different runs. The estimates are derived from the DICE model of global warming.

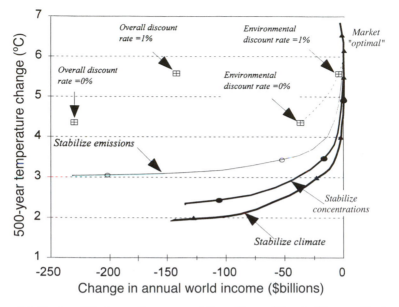

Figure 1A. Trade-off between Income and Long-Term Climate Change: Trade-off Reflecting the Alternative Policies of Table 2.

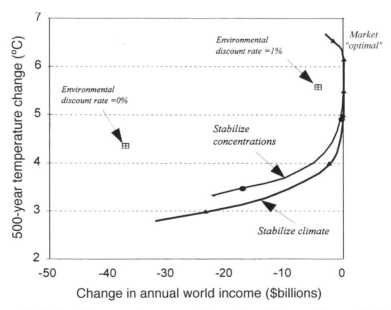

Figure 1B. Trade-off between Income and Long-Term Climate Change: Trade-off with Reduced Scale.

taken to be 3% annually, but a different annualization would only change the horizontal scale). Recall that the income variable already includes a correction for the estimated damages from climate change, but this calculation allows us to weigh the trade-off between long-term constraints on climate change (perhaps to consider "sustainable climate," to use a current cliché) and global incomes. For the long-run climate change, I have taken the increase in global mean temperature 500 years in the future to be the norm, but the results would not change appreciably if we chose 300 or 600 years.

I have also sketched in the efficiency frontier between climate change and global income with a heavy line. The line starts at the lower left by rising up and to the right for tight climate constraints; it then becomes vertical at the "optimal" climate path, and then bends backward for even higher temperature change as it passes through the "market" path which has no constraints on emissions.

Figure 1a shows all the policies considered in Table 2. The optimal climate-change policy reduces long-run global warming from 6.6 °C to 6.2 °C. Under policies that limit ultimate climate change ("stabilize climate" in Figure 1), further reductions in long-term warming to around 4.5 °C are virtually free; but when long-term temperature limitations go below around 3 °C, their cost increases sharply.

Temperature limitations are relatively efficient policies in limiting long-term warming. The question is how they compare with other proxy policies, such as ones that use differential discount rates on the environment, limit emissions or concentrations, or lower the rate of time preference and thereby raise the global savings rate. The following conclusions can be drawn from Table 2 and the figures:

- The policy of raising the savings rate (reflecting a lowering of the pure rate of social time preference from 3% to 0% or 1%) is extremely costly. Even worse, it has little effect on long-term warming. Of all the policies examined, this policy has the largest economic cost of attaining a given long-term climate objective and the least impact on long-term warming. The problem with the high-savings policy is that it requires the current generation to lower its consumption and increase its saving sharply as a means of attaining a distant environmental objective. Our calculations indicate that the net global savings rate rises from 8.1% of net global product for the 3% discount rate to 17.7% and 24.3% of output for the 1% and 0% pure rates of time preference, respectively. *In other words, the total consumption of the relatively poor current generation is taxed to increase the environmental consumption of future generations.* If there were persuasive reasons to raise global savings, this might be a sensible policy. But its requirements—to raise global savings by as much as $3 trillion today to slow global warming—is seriously out of proportion with the resources required to slow global warming.

- The use of differential discount rates for environmental investments is an interesting approach. My understanding is that this is the current practice of the U.S. Environmental Protection Agency and was recently proposed as national policy by the Council of Economic Advisers. Figure 1 shows the efficiency frontier for this policy. It is clearly less efficient than an appropriately targeted policy of limiting climate change. On the other hand, as Figure 1a shows, it is more efficient for treatment of specific long-term problems than lowering the overall discount rate on goods. It is interesting to note, however, that even with a zero environmental discount rate, long-term climate change can only be limited to about 4.3 °C.

- Figure 1a also shows that stabilizing emissions is a poor proxy for climate policy. The reason is that an efficient policy would have emissions changing over time according to the balance of costs and benefits. The policy of stabilizing emissions at 80% of 1990 levels is particularly inefficient. While it does limit ultimate warming to about 3 °C, it does so at a cost almost ten times that of the equivalent climate limitation policy.

- Stabilizing concentrations is relatively efficient. Compared to targeted climate policies, stabilizing concentrations costs around twice as much as climate stabilization. The reason is that concentrations are relatively closely linked to actual climate change.

Table 3 shows the relative efficiency of different approaches to slow long-term warming. The last column in the table shows the measure of inefficiency of a particular policy. The inefficiency measure is the cost of attaining the long-term climate objective with the policy in question compared to that of the efficient policy. The climate limitation policies are clearly efficient, while stabilizing concentrations is also relatively efficient. Ideal emissions limitations have inefficiency indexes in the single digits. Differential discount rates have considerably higher inefficiency indexes. A policy of increasing the overall savings rate has the highest inefficiency of all. (Note that in each of these, the actual policies are likely to be even more inefficient than the ideal policies shown in Table 3. For example, the Kyoto Protocol of 1997 imposes limitations only on high-income countries and excludes the developing countries. Estimates are that this failure of cost-effectiveness will raise the inefficiency index by a factor of between five and ten.)

What lesson should we draw from this analysis? *The results are sobering in that they indicate that there is no simple formula for modifying discount*

Table 3. Efficiency of Different Approaches.

Policy	Policy parameter	Rate of time preference: (percent per annum)		Relative inefficiency (1 = efficient)
		Utility	Environment	
Market	No controls	0.03	0.03	NA
Optimal		0.03	0.03	1.0
High saving		0.01	0.01	17224.6
		0.00	0.00	27790.5
Differential		0.03	0.01	409.3
discount rate		0.03	0.00	42.0
Climate target	T change < 5.5			1.0
	T change < 5	0.03	NA	1.0
	T change < 4	0.03	NA	1.0
	T change < 3	0.03	NA	1.0
	T change < 2	0.03	NA	1.0
Emission	E < E(1990)	0.03	NA	5.4
limitation	E < 0.8 E(1990)	0.03	NA	9.5
Concentration	M < 1.5 × M(0)	0.03	NA	1.7
limitation	M < 2 × M(0)	0.03	NA	1.9
	M < 3 × M(0)	0.03	NA	2.9

Note: Table shows the relative efficiency measured as the ratio of the cost of attaining the long-term climate objective with the policy under consideration compared to an efficient

rates to incorporate long-term objectives in an efficient manner. When economic analyses cannot appropriately capture all the costs and benefits, the temptation is to turn to simple solutions such as differential discount rates or intermediate objectives. Just as trade sanctions are unlikely to be a powerful weapon for human rights, so are these makeshift proxies unlikely to be efficient ways of meeting long-term objectives. We are better served by looking at the ultimate objective—in this case, global climate change—and setting our policies with this objective in mind.

For example, when we are faced with the trade-off shown in Figure 1, we might easily agree on an objective of limiting climate change to less than 4 °C, although we might become increasingly skeptical about the wisdom of tightening the limit below 3 °C. *But the dilemma of how much we should pay to slow global warming is in no way informed by the use of unrealistically low overall discount rates, or differential discount rates for environmental projects—both of which hide the underlying trade-off between the long-term objective and the economic cost.* Indeed, if we pursue our policies using inefficient tools, such as emission limitations, we might choose higher climate targets than we would if we could use efficient instruments.

What then should we conclude about discounting for the distant future? While the actual experiments conducted here strictly apply only to global warming, they are applicable to other problems that involve long-term investments where markets are defective or absent. *The main conclusion is that ad hoc manipulation of a discount rate on goods to achieve long-term goals is a very poor substitute for policies that focus directly on the ultimate objective.* Policies that distort prices are likely to produce relatively inefficient solutions, and it must be recalled that in the end the discount rate on goods is the relative price of future to present goods. Moreover, within the class of policies that distort discount rates on goods to promote long-term goals, targeted distortions in specific sectors are less harmful than distortions in the discount rates for the entire economy.

In general, targeted approaches will be more efficient ways of accomplishing long-term environmental or social objectives. The best approach will generally be to identify the long-term objectives and to take specific steps to override market decisions or conventional benefit-cost tests so as to achieve these long-term goals. Such an approach has been followed for such decisions as establishment of national parks, and it seems the more effective approach for other areas where conventional benefit-cost analysis provides unacceptable guidelines for action. *Focusing on ultimate objectives has the advantage of showing trade-offs explicitly, making the cost of violating a benefit-cost rule transparent and allowing public decisionmakers to weigh the options rather than having technicians hide the choices in complicated and abstrusely argued second-best rules of thumb.*

THREE SUMMARY RULES

It is useful to summarize these findings:

- Ad hoc manipulation of a discount rate to achieve long-term goals is a very poor substitute for policies that focus directly on the ultimate objective. Moreover, there is no simple formula for modifying discount rates that incorporates long-term objectives in an efficient manner.
- The dilemma of whether or how much to override conventional market or benefit-cost criteria is not usefully informed by the use of special, low overall or sector-specific discount rates. These merely hide the underlying trade-off between the long-term objective and the economic cost.
- Focusing on ultimate objectives has the advantage of showing trade-offs explicitly, making the cost of violating a benefit-cost rule transparent and allowing public decisionmakers to weigh the options rather than having technicians hide the choices in complicated and abstrusely argued second-best rules of thumb.

TECHNICAL APPENDIX: DETAILS OF CALCULATIONS

This appendix gives the details of the DICE model as modified for the experiments described in the paper. The sections are:

- Definitions of key variables in the DICE model
- The complete equation listing
- A description of the major experiments in the text.

Key Variables in the DICE Model

The variables are as follows. I have omitted inessential or obvious variables. In the listing, t always refers to time ($t + 1965, 1975, \ldots$).

Exogenous Variables and Parameters
$A(t)$ = level of technology
$P(t)$ = population at time t, also proportional to labor inputs
t = time
r = pure rate of social time preference

Endogenous Variables
$C(t)$ = total consumption
$c(t)$ = per capita consumption = $C(t)/P(t)$
$E(t)$ = CO_2 emissions
$F(t)$ = radiative forcing
$M(t)$ = mass of CO_2 in atmosphere
$Q(t)$ = gross world product
$T(t)$ = atmospheric temperature relative to base period
$U(t)$ = $U[c(t), P(t)]$ = utility of consumption
$Y(t)$ = gross world product (net of climate damage and mitigation costs)

Policy Variables
$I(t)$ gross investment
$\mu(t)$ = rate of emission reduction

Equations of the DICE Model

$$\underset{c(t)}{Max} = \sum_{t=0}^{T} \frac{U[c(t), P(t)]}{(1+r)^t} \tag{1}$$

subject to

$$Q(t) = A(t)K(t)^\gamma P(t)^{1-\gamma} \tag{2}$$

$$Y(t) = \Omega(t)Q(t) \tag{3}$$

$$C(t) = Y(t) - I(t) \tag{4}$$

$$E(t) = [1 - \mu(t)]\sigma(t)Q(t), \ 0 \leq \mu(t) \leq 1 \tag{5}$$

$$M(t) = M(0) + \beta E(t) + (1 - \delta_M)[M(t-1) - M(0)] \tag{6}$$

$$T(t) = T(t-1) + \frac{\tau_1[F(t) - \lambda T(t-1)] - h^*[T(t-1) - T^*(t-1)]}{\tau_2} \tag{7}$$

$$T^*(t) = T^*(t-1) + \frac{[T(t-1) - T^*(t-1)]}{\tau_3} \tag{8}$$

$$F(t) = \frac{4.1\log[M(t)/M(0)]}{\log(2)} + 0(t) \tag{9}$$

$$\Omega(t) = \frac{1 - b_1\mu(t)^{b_2}}{1 + \theta_1 T(t)^{\theta_2}} \tag{10}$$

Experiments for Discounting Analysis

The paper presents a number of different experiments to test the effects on consumption and climate change of different treatments of discounting and of alternative policies. The different experiments are as follows.

Base Run
The base run simply maximizes the objective function subject to all constraints. This run corresponds to the outcome of a standard dynamic benefit-cost analysis.

Market Runs
In the "market" runs, no emission constraints are imposed. This approach corresponds to a policy in which the climate externalities are ignored.

High Savings
The high-savings runs proceed as follows. First, the model is run with a rate of time preference of $r = 1\%$ per annum rather than 3% per annum. Then the consumption path generated by the low-discount-rate run is evaluated according to the objective function with a 3% rate of pure time preference.

Differential Discounting

For differential discounting, I first make a run for the different discount rate (being a pure rate of time preference of either 1% per annum or 0% per annum). From that run, I take the *climate policy*, represented by the trajectory of temperature change, and impose this on the model. I then reoptimize by maximizing the social welfare function with the imposed temperature trajectory and optimized consumption with the base 3% rate of time preference. In a rough sense, climate policy is chosen with the low discount rate while consumption is chosen with the base discount rate.

Emission Limitations

For emission limits, I take the model and add an equation limiting emissions.

Concentration Limitations

For concentration limits, I take the model and add an equation limiting concentrations.

Climate Targeting

For climate targeting, I impose an upper limit on the increase in global mean temperature for all periods.

Note that the "carbon taxes" in Table 2 are the dual variable of the carbon emission equation, equation (5).

ACKNOWLEDGEMENTS

I would emphasize that my thoughts in this area are drawn from a vast common intellectual property resource. I have benefited from discussions over many years with Kenneth Arrow, Robert Lind, Alan Manne, Robert Solow, James Tobin, and in an earlier era with Tjalling Koopmans.

ENDNOTES

[1]Use of market rates of return involves a number of technical issues including taxes, investment horizon, and risk: (1) The presence of taxes puts a wedge between pre-tax and post-tax returns. In such cases, the discount rate should be applied to consumption streams, and this is the approach followed in the numerical example below. (2) The discount rate may also differ by the length of the investment, with time-dependent discount rates applying to changes in consumption at different points of the future. This approach is also followed below. (3) The treatment of risk is particularly difficult because finance economists have

difficulty explaining why the risk premium on risky assets is so large (this being the "equity premium puzzle"). The assets shown in Table 1 are generally risky, so the returns there need to be corrected for risk to the extent that the investments under consideration have different risk profiles. In the area analyzed here—global warming—there are no analyses that indicate whether the payoffs from these investments have higher or lower risk (in the sense of covariance with the marginal utility of consumption) than normal investments. I therefore assume that the consumption payoffs from global warming investments have the same risk characteristics as other investments and use returns on conventional investments as the benchmark for discounting consumption flows.

[2]See William D. Nordhaus, *Managing the Global Commons*, Cambridge, Massachusetts: MIT Press, 1994.

[3]For analytical purposes, the exact value of the pure rate of time preference is irrelevant. All the qualitative results will hold if the rate is 6% or 1% rather than 3%.

16

The Implications of Hyperbolic Discounting for Project Evaluation

Maureen Cropper and David Laibson

The neoclassical theory of project evaluation (Arrow and Kurz 1970) is based on models in which agents discount the future at a constant exponential rate. There is, however, strong empirical evidence that people discount the future hyperbolically, applying larger annual discount rates to near-term returns than to returns in the distant future (Ainslie 1992; Cropper, Portney, and Aydede 1994). In this paper, we trace the implications of hyperbolic preferences for private investment choices and public policy.

The immediate problem posed by hyperbolic discounting is that it leads to time-inconsistent plans: A person who discounts the future hyperbolically will not carry out the consumption plans he makes today. From today's perspective, the discount rate between two distant periods, t and $t+1$, is a long-term low discount rate. But, when period t arrives, the individual will apply a short-term high discount rate to consumption in period $t+1$. Because it makes sense to discuss investment decisions only along consumption paths that will actually be carried out, one must begin by characterizing time-consistent plans for a consumer with hyperbolic preferences. This can be done by allowing the consumer's different temporal selves to play a game and to analyze the equilibrium of this game.

MAUREEN CROPPER is Professor of Economics at the University of Maryland, College Park; Principal Economist in the Research Department of the World Bank; and University Fellow at Resources for the Future. DAVID LAIBSON is Assistant Professor of Economics at Harvard University.

In the case of a finite-lived consumer with quasi-hyperbolic preferences, the game has a unique subgame perfect equilibrium, which (as Arrow discusses elsewhere in this volume) can be characterized by an Euler equation similar to that in the Ramsey model. The consumption path that characterizes the equilibrium of the hyperbolic consumer is thus observationally equivalent to the consumption path of a consumer who discounts the future exponentially. Moreover, the consumption rate of discount along this path should always equal the rate of return on capital. This suggests that one should discount future returns using the rate of return on capital, whether consumers have hyperbolic or exponential preferences.

This is not, however, the end of the story. As Phelps and Pollak (1968) demonstrated many years ago, the equilibrium of the game played by quasi-hyperbolic consumers is Pareto-inefficient. Consumers in all years would be better off if they each saved more, but, absent a commitment mechanism, this will never occur. This implies that there *is* a role for government policy when preferences are hyperbolic. Specifically, the government can induce Pareto improvements by subsidizing the return on capital or, equivalently, by lowering the required rate of return on investment projects. Calibration of the hyperbolic model implies that the magnitude of this subsidy should be about two percentage points annually.

We hasten to add that this conclusion does not favor environmental projects vis-à-vis other forms of investment. Hyperbolic preferences provide a motive for lowering the required return on *all* capital investment projects because of the undersaving that occurs along the hyperbolic equilibrium path, but do not favor one type of capital over another.

The remainder of the paper is organized as follows. The next section introduces the notion of hyperbolic preferences. The subsequent section describes the intertemporal game played by a consumer with quasi-hyperbolic preferences and characterizes the equilibrium of that game. The third section adds a government to the model of the second section, and the fourth and final section brings these arguments together in our concluding remarks.

HYPERBOLIC DISCOUNTING AND ITS CONSEQUENCES

The neoclassical theory of optimal growth assumes that people have stationary time preferences: that the choice between two payoffs depends only on the absolute time interval separating them. There is, however, strong empirical evidence that people are more sensitive to a given time delay if it occurs closer to the present than if it occurs farther in the future (Ainslie 1992; Cropper, Portney, and Aydede 1994). In other words, the discount rate that applies to near-term consumption trade-offs is higher than the discount rate that applies to long-term consumption trade-offs. Loewenstein and Prelec (1992) present an axiomatic analysis of such preferences, which implies a generalized hyperbolic discount function, that is, a function of the form

$$\phi(t) = (1 + \alpha t)^{-\gamma/\alpha}, \; \alpha, \gamma > 0 \tag{1}$$

As $\alpha \to 0$, $\phi(t)$ approaches the exponential function. When α is very large, $\phi(t)$ approximates a step function, implying that all periods after the first receive approximately equal weight. For $\alpha > 0$, $\phi(t)$ lies below the exponential function at low t and above it at high t.

In what follows, we approximate the hyperbolic function with a quasi-hyperbolic function, first proposed by Phelps and Pollak (1968) for intergenerational analysis and then applied by Laibson (1997) for intrapersonal analysis. Specifically, we examine a representative consumer who lives T periods and whose period t self receives utility from the consumption sequence $(c_0, c_1, \ldots, c_T)$ according to

$$U_t(c_0, c_1, \ldots, c_T) = u(c_t) + \beta \sum_{i=1}^{T-t} \delta^i u(c_{t+i}), \quad 0 < \beta, \delta < 1 \tag{2}$$

When $0 < \beta < 1$, the discount structure in equation (2) mimics the qualitative properties of the hyperbolic function, while maintaining most of the analytical tractability of the exponential discount function. We shall refer to the discount factors $\{1, \beta\delta, \beta\delta^2, \beta\delta^3, \ldots\}$ as quasi-hyperbolic. Figure 1 graphs the exponential discount function for $\delta = 0.97$, the hyperbolic discounting function with $\alpha = 10^5$ and $\gamma = 5 \times 10^3$, and the quasi-hyperbolic discounting function with $\beta = 0.6$ and $\delta = 0.99$.

To illustrate the time-inconsistency problems to which quasi-hyperbolic preferences give rise, consider what happens if self 0 chooses the consumption sequence $(c_0, c_1, \ldots, c_T)$ to maximize equation (2) subject to the constraints (3) and (4),

$$0 \leq c_t \leq W_t \tag{3}$$

$$W_{t+1} = R \cdot (W_t - c_t) \tag{4}$$

where W_t is period t wealth and R is the gross return on capital. As Strotz (1955) first pointed out, the consumption levels $(c_1, c_2, \ldots, c_T)$ chosen by self 0 will not be followed by future selves if they are free to choose their consumption levels. From self 0's perspective, the discount rate between

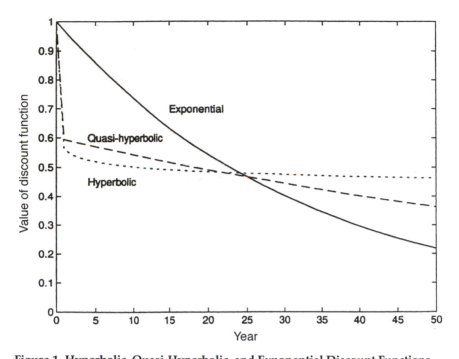

Figure 1. Hyperbolic, Quasi-Hyperbolic, and Exponential Discount Functions.

Note: This figure graphs the hyperbolic discounting function with $\alpha = 10^5$ and $\gamma = 5 \times 10^3$, the quasi-hyperbolic discounting function with $\beta = 0.6$ and $\delta = 0.99$, and the exponential discount function for $\delta = 0.97$.

two distant periods, t and $t+1$, is a long-term low discount rate. But self t will discount consumption in period $t+1$ at a much higher rate. Self t will, therefore, consume more and save less than self 0 would have chosen for him.

To analyze a set of consumption plans that all future selves would actually follow, we examine the equilibrium of an intertemporal game first analyzed by Phelps and Pollak (1968).

THE EQUILIBRIUM OF A GAME WITH
QUASI-HYPERBOLIC CONSUMERS

Consider the decision problem of a consumer with a finite lifetime ($t = 0, 1, \ldots, T$). Suppose that self t of the consumer has control over the period t consumption decision. We assume that self t observes all past consumption levels ($c_0, c_1, c_2, \ldots, c_{t-1}$) and current wealth, W_t and chooses consumption in period t, c_t, subject to the budget constraint (3). Self $t+1$ inherits wealth W_{t+1}, according to equation (4), and similarly chooses c_{t+1}. The payoff that self t receives is given by equation (2), where $u(c)$ is a member of the class of constant relative risk aversion (CRRA) utility functions

$$u(c) = \frac{c^{1-\rho} - 1}{1-\rho}, \quad \infty > \rho > 0 \tag{5}$$

Consider now the equilibria of this game. As Laibson has shown (1996), when T is finite, the game played by different temporal selves has a unique subgame perfect equilibrium. Each self's equilibrium consumption strategy is a linear function of its inherited wealth, $c_t = \lambda_t W_t$, and the consumption path is characterized by

$$u'(c_t) = R\delta u'(c_{t+1})[\lambda_{t+1}(\beta - 1) + 1] \tag{6}$$

where $\lambda_{t+1} = \partial c_{t+1}(W_{t+1}, T)/\partial W_{t+1}$. As $T \to \infty$, equation (6) converges to

$$u'(c_t) = R\delta u'(c_{t+1})[\lambda^*(\beta - 1) + 1] \tag{6a}$$

where λ^* is the solution to the nonlinear equation

$$\lambda^* = 1 - (\delta R^{1-\rho})^{1/\rho}[\lambda^*(\beta - 1) + 1]^{1/\rho} \tag{7}$$

When $\beta = 1$, equation (6a) is identical to the condition that characterizes the optimal consumption path in the Ramsey model. Even when $\beta \neq 1$, there is still an observational equivalence result noted by Arrow (this volume), between the equilibrium of the game with quasi-hyperbolic preferences and the Ramsey model. Specifically, the consumption path corresponding to equation (6a) is identical to the consumption path generated by a Ramsey model in which utility is discounted at the constant exponential rate $\underline{\delta} = \delta[\lambda^*(\beta-1) + 1]$.

In contrast to the Ramsey model, however, the consumption path that characterizes the game with quasi-hyperbolic preferences is not Pareto-efficient. As Phelps and Pollak (1968) first pointed out, all selves would be better off if they all consumed less than the equilibrium consumption rate, but there is no mechanism to guarantee that this strategy will be followed.[1] The intuition behind this result is simple. While requiring self t to save more lowers self t's utility, requiring all other selves to save more raises self t's utility, and the second effect dominates the first. This suggests that it may be possible for the government to enact policies to increase saving that will be Pareto-improving.

PARETO-IMPROVING GOVERNMENT POLICIES
IN A QUASI-HYPERBOLIC WORLD

In a world in which consumers can be made better off by lowering the fraction of wealth that they consume, there are two ways that the government can improve welfare. One is to subsidize interest rates (raise R to $\hat{R}$); the other is to penalize consumption. Laibson (1996) focuses on both strategies. Here, we consider only interest rate subsidies.

We model the government as a sequence of players $\{0,1,2,...,T\}$ who can tax consumers and use the proceeds to subsidize interest rates. An essential feature of each government is that it can implement policies only with a lag: due to delays in the budget process, government t picks the lump-sum tax in period $t+1$, τ_{t+1}, and $\hat{R}_{t+1} - R$, the interest rate subsidy in period $t+1$.[2] The effect of this assumption is to give the government a commitment technology. The time t government cannot instantaneously overturn the policies of the time $t-1$ government. In this way, the government is able to overcome the self-control problem that plagues consumers.

The goal of the government at time t is to maximize the well-being of self t. The government's policy instrument influences marginal trade-offs between periods $t+1$ and $t+2$. Between $t+1$ and $t+2$, the time t government would ideally like the consumption path to be

$$u'(c_{t+1}) = \delta R u'(c_{t+2}) \tag{8}$$

where R is the unsubsidized marginal rate of transformation. Note that β does not appear in this equation, as δ is the relevant discount factor between periods $t+1$ and $t+2$ from government t's perspective. Equation (8) implies

$$\left(\frac{c_{t+2}}{c_{t+1}}\right)^{\rho} = \delta R \tag{9}$$

The time t government can implement this path by choosing an interest subsidy $\hat{R} = \hat{R}_{t+1}$, such that the generalized Euler equation (with subsidized interest rate) is consistent with the government's desired consumption path,

$$\left(\frac{c_{t+2}}{c_{t+1}}\right)^{\rho} = \delta \hat{R}[\lambda^*(\hat{R})(\beta-1)+1] \tag{10}$$

where $\lambda^*(\hat{R})$ is the value of λ^* implied by equation (7) when R is replaced by $\hat{R}$. Equations (9) and (10) jointly imply that the time t government picks $\hat{R}$ such that

$$\delta R = \delta\hat{R}[\lambda^*(\hat{R})(\beta-1)+1] \tag{11}$$

This argument holds for all governments (that is, for all times t). So, in equilibrium $\hat{R}_{t+1} = \hat{R}$ for all $t \geq 0$.

To solve explicitly for the interest rate subsidy as a function of model parameters, we rely on the fact that $c_{t+s} = \lambda^*(\hat{R})W_{t+s}$, for all $s \geq 1$. Together with equation (4), this implies that

$$\frac{c_{t+s+1}}{c_{t+s}} = [1-\lambda^*(\hat{R})]\hat{R} \tag{12}$$

Inserting equation (12) into equation (9) yields $\lambda^*(\hat{R})$ as a function of R and $\hat{R}$,

$$\left([1-\lambda^*(\hat{R})]\hat{R}\right)^{\rho} = \delta R \tag{13}$$

which, together with equation (11) yields the interest rate subsidy as a function of model parameters

$$\hat{R} - R = \left((1-\beta)[1-(\delta R^{1-\rho})]^{1/\rho}\right)\left(\frac{R}{\beta}\right) \tag{14}$$

To illustrate the magnitude of the interest subsidy, we consider plausible values for the parameters of the quasi-hyperbolic discounting function, β and δ, the gross returns on capital, R, and the elasticity of marginal utility with respect to consumption, ρ. Suppose that $\rho = 3$ and $R = \exp(.04)$, that is, the gross return on capital is 4%. The values $\beta = 0.6$ and $\delta = 0.99$ pictured in Figure 1 are roughly consistent with empirical evidence on intertemporal choices presented by Ainslie (1992). Together, these parameters imply an interest rate subsidy of more than two percentage points ($\hat{R} - R = 0.021$).

We note that this subsidy puts the economy on a Pareto-efficient path. The equilibrium path that arises in the game with government is identical to the consumption path that would be chosen by self 0 if self 0 could commit all future selves. Note that on the equilibrium, path $u'(c_t) = \delta R u'(c_{t+1})$ for all $t > 0$. This is exactly the equilibrium path self 0 would like to implement. Hence, the equilibrium path is Pareto-efficient, as any perturbation to the path would make self 0 worse off.

CONCLUSIONS

When agents discount future utility of consumption using a quasi-hyper-bolic rather than an exponential function, the equilibrium consumption path in the economy is no longer Pareto-efficient. All consumers would be better off if they each saved more, but there is no way to coordinate this behavior. This suggests a role for government policy: by subsidizing interest rates (reducing the required return on investment projects), the government can help to overcome the self-control problem that results from hyperbolic preferences.

As we noted in the introduction, however, this is not a pro-environ-ment result. It does not justify applying a lower discount rate to an envi-ronmental project (for example, a reforestation project) than would be applied to the building of a steel mill. Are there assumptions that would justify such a practice? The answer is yes. In a world of quasi-hyperbolic preferences, one can justify applying a lower discount rate to environ-mental projects under the following three conditions:

- the production of environmental services (Y^E) from an environmental capital stock (E)—for example, a forest—is a separate process from the production of private output (Y) from private capital (K) (separa-bility in production);
- the environmental consumption good (c^E) and the private consump-tion good (c) are imperfect substitutes in the utility function (separa-bility in consumption); and
- the government controls the rate of consumption of the environmen-tal good and, as is assumed above, the government can act only with a lag—in period t it chooses the amount of the environmental good that will be consumed in period $t+1$ (c^E_{t+1}).[3]

Under these conditions, one can show that the government will choose to consume a lower fraction of the environmental capital stock than consumers will choose to consume out of private capital, and that the steady-state rate of return on environmental capital will lie below the return on private capital. Thus, a lower discount rate should be applied to environmental projects than to private investments. The intuition behind this result is as follows. As long as the government can act only with a lag, it is prevented from overconsuming the environmental good, as con-sumers are tempted to do in the case of a private good. Furthermore, because of the assumed lack of substitutability between the environmental good and other goods, both in production and in consumption, consumers cannot undo the government's choices.

This result is, however, a fragile one: it will fail to hold if any one of the three assumptions listed earlier is violated. In particular, if there is substitutability in production or consumption between the environmental good and other goods, the same rate of return will apply to both environmental and nonenvironmental capital. This underscores the main point of this paper. While hyperbolic discounting provides a rationale for lowering the required rate of return on investment projects, it does not provide justification for those who seek to treat environmental projects differently from other investment projects.

ENDNOTES

[1]This can be seen as follows. Write self t's utility as a function of λ^*, the fraction of wealth consumed in the long run:

$$U_t(\lambda^*) = u(\lambda^* W_t) + \beta\delta u[\lambda^*(1-\lambda^*)RW_t] + \beta\delta^2 u[\lambda^*(1-\lambda^*)^2 R^2 W_t] + \beta\delta^3 u[\lambda^*(1-\lambda^*)^3 R^3 W_t] + \dots$$

Phelps and Pollak showed that $\partial U_t(\lambda^*)/\partial\lambda^* < 0$.

[2]Since the consumers in this economy are not liquidity-constrained, the timing of lump-sum taxes is irrelevant. We therefore focus on the choice of interest rate subsidy.

[3]Formally, suppose that

$$Y_t = A_t K_t{}^\alpha \quad 0 \le c_t \le K_t \qquad\qquad K_t = (1-d)K_{t-1} + Y_t - c_t$$
$$Y^E{}_t = A_t E_t{}^\alpha \quad 0 \le c^E{}_t \le E_t \qquad\qquad E_t = (1-d)E_{t-1} + Y^E{}_t - c^E{}_t$$

The preferences of self t and government t are given by

$$v(c^E_t, c_t) + \beta\delta \sum_{i=1}^{T-t} \delta^i v(c^E_{t+1}, c_{t+i})$$

REFERENCES

Ainslie, George W. 1992. *Picoeconomics*. Cambridge: Cambridge University Press.

Arrow, Kenneth J., and Mordecai Kurz. 1970. *Public Investment, The Rate of Return and Optimal Fiscal Policy*. Baltimore: Johns Hopkins University Press for Resources for the Future.

Cropper, Maureen L., Sema K. Aydede, and Paul R. Portney. 1994. Preferences for Life Saving Programs: How the Public Discounts Time and Age. *Journal of Risk and Uncertainty* 8: 243–65.

Laibson, David I. 1996. *Hyperbolic Discount Functions, Undersaving, and Savings Policy.* NBER Working Paper 5635. June. Cambridge, Massachusetts: National Bureau of Economic Research, Inc.

———. 1997. Golden Eggs and Hyperbolic Discounting. *Quarterly Journal of Economics* 112: 443–77.

Loewenstein, George, and Drazen Prelec. 1992. Anomalies in Intertemporal Choice: Evidence and an Interpretation. *Quarterly Journal of Economics* 107: 573–98.

Phelps, E. S., and R. A. Pollak. 1968. On Second-Best National Saving and Game: Equilibrium Growth. *Review of Economic Studies* 35: 185–99.

Strotz, Robert H. 1955. Myopia and Inconsistency in Dynamic Utility Maximization. *Review of Economic Studies* 23: 165–80.

17

Analysis for Intergenerational Decisionmaking

Robert C. Lind

This workshop has already become known as the workshop on discounting, but if one reads the charge to the participants, it is clearly much more than that. In fact, the focus on the procedure of discounting and the choice of a specific rate in many ways distracts us from the nature of the major choices that people and societies face and the methodological issues that the analysis of these choices raises. The first and fourth questions raised by Paul Portney and John Weyant are—in analyzing public investments or policies, where the costs and benefits occur over centuries—whether we can use the standard benefit-cost methodology that has been used for years in public investment and policy analysis, and whether we can use the net present value of benefits as a basis for making public policy decisions. Further, if we can do so, what is the appropriate rate of discount that, as we know, frequently drives the outcome of the analysis where there are long time horizons? The followup questions are: if we cannot use the standard benefit-cost methodology, how then should these long-lived public investment and policy choices be analyzed and evaluated and, in particular, what is the role for discounting in any new approach to the evaluation of public investments and policies?

My responses to these questions are mixed in that I believe investments and policies that span centuries do present some significant differences, at least in degree, from their standard shorter-term counterparts that require changes in the way we evaluate them. On the other hand, I

ROBERT C. LIND is Professor of Economics, Management, and Public Policy at Cornell University's Johnson Graduate School of Management.

believe that many aspects of benefit-cost analysis are still important to the evaluation of these projects and policies. I also believe that models employing discounting can be very informative to the evaluation process, particularly in measuring the opportunity costs associated with various options.

On the other hand, I do not believe that a decision such as whether to go forward with a program to mitigate global warming can be made on the basis of a decision model that projects future costs and benefits and discounts them to a present value using any rate of discount. In this regard, I am in agreement with Thomas Schelling that the fundamental choice is whether to transfer resources from the present and near-term future generations to generations living in the distant future that may be better off or worse off, and an exponential discount rate or a market rate of interest is largely irrelevant to making this ethical decision. Further, I believe this decision requires more information than is often contained in a discounted cash flow analysis, such as how rich are current generations compared with future generations? This means, in particular, that I reject the arguments associated with the approaches to choosing a discount rate based on a utilitarian welfare function as set forth in optimal growth models. A corollary to this is that these models and this mode of analysis cannot tell us what the optimal policy with regard to climate mitigation is either.

To understand the bases for these positions it is important first to lay out what I believe are some of the major differences between investment and policy decisions that have long horizons where many generations are affected and those that are relatively short, and to spell out the implications of these differences for public investment and policy analysis and evaluation. As part of this analysis, I will present what I consider the primary case against the rationale for an exponential discount rate based on optimal growth theory. Then, I raise what I believe is one of the most difficult unresolved problems for the analysis of projects with long horizons, and in particular global warming: the characterization and measurement of the opportunity costs associated with displacing higher-yield private and alternative public investments.

MAJOR DIFFERENCES BETWEEN POLICY CHOICES WITH VERY LONG HORIZONS AND INVESTMENTS WITH RELATIVELY SHORT HORIZONS

When projects span many generations, consideration of the distribution of both consumption and utility across these generations becomes significant and the discounted sum of either consumption or utility does not capture our concern for this distribution. Furthermore, intergenerational transfers, either forward or backward, generally must be made through series of intervening generations. Designing and implementing such transfers is virtually impossible, and the potential for an intervening generation to break the chain of transfer makes such transfer schemes virtually impossible to implement (Lind 1995). In benefit-cost terms, this means that it is impossible for the beneficiaries to pay compensation to those incurring the costs. Therefore, future generations that would enjoy the benefits of climate mitigation cannot compensate near-term generations that will pay the costs, nor can the present generation choose not to mitigate and compensate distant future generations by investing the savings—from choosing not to mitigate—at a market rate of return and bestow the accumulated wealth on distant future generations to compensate them for the costs they will incur from climate change. Therefore, compensation cannot be paid in either direction and this negates the logic behind the compensation test that is the foundation of the benefit-cost criterion. A further implication for the analysis and evaluation of long-term projects and policies of our inability to plan and implement intergenerational transfers is that we need to display the time profiles of consumption and other variables and not just display present values.

A second difference associated with long intergenerational projects is that there is a much higher level of uncertainty about everything—from people's tastes to their incomes, to technology, and to the state of the planet. It is simply impossible to do more than intelligently speculate on the future of the planet two centuries from now. What this implies for policy analysis and evaluation is that we must take a sequential approach that involves changing and updating our policies as new information becomes available. There are at least three important reasons for delaying decisions under these circumstances. First, by waiting we will have better information; second, by waiting we will have improved technical options for addressing a problem; and third, we can use the resources we would have spent for other valuable activities or investments. In this context, each policy decision positions us to make the next policy decision later. Policy action is akin to buying an option to facilitate future action. The case for immediate action is generated by the existence of irreversabilities. Again, this can best be analyzed in a sequential decision framework. Taking action now to prevent irreversible effects is like buying an option (Dixit and Pindyck 1994). While I believe this type of sequential analysis and decision making is also appropriate for analyzing many shorter-term investments, it is critical for analyzing investments that span centuries.

In the case of climate change, given that the near-term generations who will pay the costs cannot be compensated by future generations, any expenditure now for mitigation is a transfer from near-term generations to those in the distant future. As Schelling (1995) correctly notes, it must be analyzed as a gift to someone else, not as an investment for one's own future consumption. Therefore, the appropriate question for weighing costs and benefits in a dynamic decision process is, how much are people willing to pay today for the knowledge (a benefit to them) that we will have certain options open for dealing with climate change in the future given the information and technology available to society in the future?

This is a different concept of the relevant costs and benefits than in the traditional benefit-cost paradigm. This does not mean that estimating the standard costs and benefits accruing into the future is not important. It is very important, as dynamic optimization techniques demonstrate to us. What we are willing to pay to preserve or create options at some point in the future will depend in large part on the potential net benefits in the future that having these options will generate. However, this approach suggests that the standard benefit-cost methodology of trying to predict the future the best that we can, estimating costs and benefits over time the best that we can, making the appropriate adjustments for risk (which we never do), then discounting costs and benefits to their present value, and finally deciding to undertake a policy based on whether this present value is positive—or, in the case of several options, choosing the one with the highest positive net present value—is neither the way to formulate the problem nor does it provide a defensible basis for a policy choice.

To illustrate this, consider the following hypothetical cases. We today are faced with two investment options that will benefit people living 200 and 300 years from now, respectively. This is a pure transfer from the present to the future. Further, assume through all time the marginal rate of return on alternative private and public investments is 10%. The first investment being considered will earn a certain internal rate of return of 0%, well below the 10%, and will benefit people living 200 years from now who, we know with certainty, will be on the verge of starvation and so the proposed program will save them. The preferred decision may well be to make that investment and transfer the resources to the future generation even though it earns a zero rate of return. At this point an eager graduate student jumps up, sensing an economic slam dunk, and says, "That was a really dumb decision. You could have invested that money at 10% and made those people a lot better off." Wrong! We don't know how to set aside investment funds and to commit intervening generations to investing and reinvesting those funds for eventual delivery as consumer goods to the generation 200 years from now.

Now take the second policy to undertake an investment that will transfer resources to a generation living 300 years from now. This investment has an internal rate of return of 20%. However, the current generation knows that the generation living 300 years from now will be 100 times wealthier than it is and, in a no-brainer, decides not to make this investment. Our graduate student seeking redemption jumps up and says, "Why doesn't the current generation undertake the investment and have the future generation transfer an amount equal to a 15% return back to it and let the future generation keep the rest so both will be better off?" In theory, this could be done in a world with overlapping generations. In practice, this is virtually impossible, in part because of the problem of getting and enforcing the commitment of intervening generations to carry out this intergenerational transfer. The logic of the benefit-cost criterion, in the absence of an explicit social welfare function, rests on our ability to make income transfers through time along a budget line involving some rate of return, and when that cannot be done, the logic behind the net present value criterion does not hold. We are so used to assuming the ability to transfer resources over time we sometimes forget that if we can't, then it is not appropriate to convert all flows to a present value.

One line of argument in support of using a net present value calculation that does not require our being able to make intergenerational transfers is to introduce a specific social welfare function as is done in the optimal growth models. Then economists appeal to the conditions on the optimal growth path, that is, $i = r = \text{SRTP} = \rho + \theta g$ where i is the marginal rate of return on capital, r is the rate of discount with respect to consumption, SRTP represents the social rate of time preference, ρ equals the utility rate of discount, θ is the absolute value of the elasticity of marginal utility, and g is the growth rate of per capita income (IPPC 1996, Chapter 4).

There are two variations on how this equation is interpreted. One is to use the left side of the equation and to set $\text{SRTP} = i$ or the marginal rate of return on capital and to use that as the discount rate. The second is to assert that intergenerational equity requires that utility of each generation be given equal weight and therefore, ρ, the utility rate of discount should be zero so the SRTP is equal to θg. Then, estimates or assumptions are made about the values of θ and g to arrive at a discount rate. I have many problems with this latter approach that I have expressed elsewhere (Lind 1995). But there are problems with both approaches as they are based on a utilitarian ethical system that is built into the growth model, but that certainly is not well understood or accepted by people generally or elected decisionmakers in particular. Further, the utilitarian ethical framework implies that society should be making choices that it does not in fact make, that is, equalizing incomes within a given generation. In the case of intertemporal allocation, it in some cases implies that we should be transferring resources from poorer near-term generations to richer future generations. The problem is not that the utilitarian framework is in some absolute sense wrong. It is that it is neither well understood nor accepted by elected decisionmakers, and it implies that we should take actions that are totally inconsistent with the choices our society actually makes. For economists to introduce such an ethical system, to use it as a basis for discounting and the choice of a discount rate in evaluating long-term public investments, and then to present the results as science without painstakingly spelling out the ethical system embodied in these results is at the very least overreaching the limits of what we can as economists tell policymakers about what policies they should pursue, and some might be much less charitable about characterizing this behavior.

OPPORTUNITY COST

When considering public investments in which the costs and benefits span centuries, there is another analytical problem that becomes more difficult, namely characterizing and measuring the opportunity cost of undertaking that investment. A long-standing concern relating to the choice of the discount rate in benefit-cost analysis is that one doesn't want to undertake low rate of return public investments that will displace either higher-yield private investments or alternative public investments.

Assume that a one dollar investment in the mitigation of climate change had an internal rate of return of 3% over a 300-year horizon. If there were private or other public investments with, say, a 5% internal rate of return with the same time profile over 300 years, one would want to undertake these higher-yield investments before investing in mitigation. The problem is that there aren't many investments regardless of their internal rate of return that have anything like a 300-year horizon.

Most investments are much shorter. To simplify, let's assume that these investments are one year in length and earn 5%; thus, one dollar invested today pays $1.05 in one year. Now suppose that one dollar of investment in mitigation displaces one dollar of private investment that earns 5%. Further, let us assume again for simplicity that the 3% internal rate of return for 300 years is generated by a process where one dollar is invested and returns 3% each year and that the principal plus the accumulated interest are reinvested each year for 300 years. Clearly, if we could put together a series of one-year 5% investments where the principal and interest were reinvested it would considerably dominate the investment in mitigation. However, when we displace a one-dollar, one-year private investment by a one-dollar, 300-year public investment, the opportunity cost can differ greatly depending on one's assumption of the reinvestment process in the private sector. If the $1.05 returned at the end of one year is treated as ordinary income (and assuming the marginal propensity to save is 0.20), then only $.20 is reinvested at 5% the next year, whereas if the original one dollar invested is treated as a return of capital and reinvested and 20% of the interest is reinvested, the investment at 5% in the second period would be $1.01. In the first case, the amount reinvested in the private sector in the second year is significantly less than if there were full reinvestment of the principal and interest, and in the second case it is only slightly less. How one models this investment and reinvestment process significantly affects the opportunity cost of displacing investments with higher returns but much shorter lives in the private or public sector. This issue is related to the shadow price of capital (Bradford 1975, Lind 1982).

In the case of climate-change analysis, most of the studies employ neoclassical economic growth models. I have suggested to the modeling community at a previous conference that one way of showing the potential opportunity costs of displacing private investment as a result of mitigation would be to run the growth model with mitigation investment and then to run the model assuming the investment in mitigation had all been put into higher-yield alternative investments. The next step would be to compare the two consumption streams generated by the runs. The difference would represent the opportunity cost or benefit of mitigation. One modeler, William Nordhaus, who is on this panel, reported to me that he made such a model run and, if I understand him correctly, the difference was lost in the rounding error of the model's output. What this tells me is either that the opportunity cost is not that significant or that the fact that growth models essentially treat investment as returning the principle and interest associated with investment in the next period as ordinary income that is then divided between saving and investment results in the understatement of this cost of displacing a higher-yield investment with one with a lower yield.

Why is this important? The major criticism by me and by others of investment in mitigation that has a relatively low internal rate of return is that it will displace, or alternatively could have been channeled in to, very high-yield alternative investments. Most often mentioned are investments yielding 20% to 40% such as education or public health in developing countries. The question is, how do we quantify these costs and how significant are they? I believe we should look at this by determining the impact of the displacement or the consumption stream. I hope more modelers will perform this experiment with their models.

CONCLUDING REMARKS

In conclusion, having said that we cannot tell whether we should invest in such long-term policies as the mitigation of climate change based on the calculation of the present value of net benefits given any discount rate, what should we do? Should we throw away our models that incorporate discounting? Of course not, but we should recognize that while they can be very informative and instructive as to the trade-offs we face, they do not provide a complete basis for decision making or for determining what is an optimal policy. Second, because these investments span many generations, it is important for the modelers to display the time paths of variables, not just present values. This is particularly true for consumption over time. Modelers need to systematically explore the opportunity cost of investing in, say, mitigation instead of shorter investments with higher internal rates of return by plotting the two alternative consumption streams and looking at their difference. That done, I wouldn't even mind converting these differences to a present value using several different discount rates.

I believe the way we analyze very big long-term investment projects such as climate change mitigation requires some substantial adjustments in the way we go about analyzing and evaluating our options from the procedures we use in performing standard benefit-cost analysis on relatively small short-term public investment today. In particular, the analysis should be sequential. I believe this will evolve as we face and grapple with long-term issues such as climate change.

REFERENCES

Bradford, D. F. 1975. Constraints on Government Investment Opportunities and the Choice of Discount Rate. *American Economic Review* 65(50): 887–99.

Cline, W. R. 1992. *The Economics of Global Warming.* Washington, D.C.: Institute for International Economics.

Dixit, A. K., and R. S. Pindyck. 1994. *Investment Under Uncertainty.* Princeton: Princeton University Press.

IPCC (Intergovernmental Panel on Climate Change). 1996. *Climate Change 1995: Economic and Social Dimensions of Climate Change. The Contribution of Working Group III to the Second Assessment Report of the Intergovernmental Panel on Climate Change.* Edited by J. P. Bruce, H. Lee, and E. F. Haites. Cambridge: Cambridge University Press.

Lind, R. C. 1982. A Primer on the Major Issues Relating to the Discount Rate for Evaluating National Energy Options. In R. C. and others, *Discounting for Time and Risk in Energy Policy.* Washington, D.C.: Resources for the Future/Johns Hopkins University Press.

———. 1995. Intergenerational Equity, Discounting, and the Role of Benefit-Cost Analysis in Evaluating Global Climate Policy. *Energy Policy* 23(4/5): 379–89.

Rawls, J. 1971. *A Theory of Justice.* Cambridge, Massachusetts: Harvard University Press.

Schelling, T. C. 1995. Intergenerational Discounting. *Energy Policy* 23(4/5): 395–401.

Index